# Myth and Paradox of the Single Market

# Myth and Paradox of the Single Market

How the trade benefits of EU membership
have been mis-sold

**Michael Burrage**

CIVITAS

First Published January 2016

© Civitas 2016
55 Tufton Street
London SW1P 3QL

email: books@civitas.org.uk

ISBN 978-1-906837-75-4

Designed and typeset by
lukejefford.com

Printed in Great Britain by
Berforts Ltd
Hastings, TN35 4NR

# Contents

# Author

**Michael Burrage** is a director of Cimigo, which is based in Ho Chi Minh City, Vietnam, and conducts market and corporate strategy research in China, India and 12 countries in the Asia Pacific region. He is also a founder director of a start-up specialist telecom company which provides the free telephone interpreter service for aid workers and others where interpreters are scarce.

He is a sociologist by training, was a Fulbright scholar at the University of Pennsylvania, has been a lecturer at the London School of Economics and at the Institute of United States Studies, specialising in the comparative analysis of industrial enterprise and professional institutions. He has been a research fellow at Harvard, at the Swedish Collegium of Advanced Study, Uppsala, at the Free University of Berlin, and at the Center for Higher Education Studies and the Institute of Government of the University of California, Berkeley. He has also been British Council lecturer at the University of Pernambuco, Recife, Brazil, and on several occasions a visiting professor in Japan, at the universities of Kyoto, Hokkaido and Kansai and at Hosei University in Tokyo.

He has written articles in American, European and Japanese sociological journals, conducted a comparative study of telephone usage in Tokyo, Manhattan, Paris and London for NTT, and a study of British entrepreneurs for Ernst & Young. His publications include *Revolution and the Making of the Contemporary Legal Profession: England, France and the United States* (OUP, 2006) and *Class Formation, Civil Society and the State: A comparative analysis of Russia, France, the United States and England* (Palgrave Macmillan, 2008). He edited Martin Trow: Twentieth-century higher education: from elite to mass to universal (Johns Hopkins, 2010).

His previous Civitas publications include *Where's the Insider Advantage? A review of the evidence that withdrawal from the EU would not harm the UK's exports or foreign investment in the UK* (July 2014) and 'A club of high and severe unemployment: the Single Market over the 21 years 1993-2013' (July 2015) in the Europe Debate series.

# Acknowledgements

I have benefited greatly from the statistical savvy of Nigel Williams, from the deep understanding of the EU of Jonathan Lindsell, from the insightful observations of a blind reviewer, and from the editorial forbearance and judgement of Daniel Bentley. They all did their best, and I cannot, alas, blame any of them for any errors that might remain. They are all my own work.

# Summary

Claims are frequently made about the benefits of the Single Market for UK trade. The investigation that follows was provoked by one of the more astonishing, made to parliament in 2011 by Ed Davey, then minister of state at the Department for Business, Innovation and Skills (BIS), that 'EU countries trade twice as much with each other as they would do in the absence of the Single Market programme'. It examines the evidence provided by BIS, in response to a freedom of information request, which was supposed to justify his claim.

None of it did so. At that time, the government had evidently collected no data to show what the trade benefits of the Single Market might be for the UK, and the minister and his department relied on research provided some years before by three French academics and, more importantly, on a 2007 European Commission report which had listed many failings of the Single Market in an attempt to make the case for further European integration.

BIS also referred to two other sources of evidence that post-dated the minister's claim, as if it might vindicate him retrospectively. One was a volume the department had itself published, but this included no reliable evidence on the benefits of the Single Market. The other was the Review of the Balance of Competences between the UK and the EU, which was conducted by the Foreign Office. This included claims by the CBI, TheCityUK and various trade federations and businesses that UK exporters have benefited by ceding responsibility for trade negotiations to the EC. None of them cited any systematic or reliable evidence to support the minister's claim.

To evaluate it, the free trade agreements concluded by the EU are compared here with those negotiated by Chile, Korea, Singapore and Switzerland, four independent countries which have none of the 'heft' or 'clout' or 'negotiating leverage' which the CBI and many businesses consider essential in trade negotiations. The conclusions are:

- Since 1970, the EC has concluded 36 agreements, most of them with small economies, some multi-country. The aggregate GDP in 2015 of the 55 countries with an EU agreement in force in January 2015 is $6.7tn, which is only slightly more than the $6tn GDP of Japan.

- By contrast the aggregate GDP of all the countries with which Chile had agreements in force is $58.3tn, Korea's totalled $40.8tn, Singapore's $38.7tn and Switzerland's $39.8tn. However, the agreements of these four countries include their agreements with the EU, which has a GDP of $16.7tn.

- About 90 per cent of the agreements of these four smaller, independent countries include services, whereas only 68 per cent of the EC's trade agreements do so.

- The EC has therefore opened services markets of just $4.8tn to UK exporters, whereas the Swiss have opened markets of $35tn, the Singaporeans of $37.2tn, the Koreans of $40tn and Chileans of $55.4tn. However, we do not know if the EC agreements secured better terms than these independent countries, since the scope of these agreements has never been compared in detail.

- Analysis of the growth of UK exports of goods before and after EC agreements have come into force, for at least five years, shows that in most cases (10 out of 15) the post-agreement growth of UK exports has fallen. The five countries where the post-agreement growth of UK exports rose were Turkey, Chile, Lebanon, Papua New Guinea and Fiji. These therefore are the clear success stories of 42 years of EC negotiation on the UK's behalf. Their total GDP in 2015 was $1.1tn, which is significantly less than the $1.5tn GDP of Australia with which the EC has yet to negotiate an agreement.

- By contrast most of Switzerland's agreements (11 out of 15), most of Singapore's (eight out of 12) and most of Korea's (four out of five) have been followed by an increase in the rate of growth of their exports to the partner countries. Most Chilean agreements (13 out of 18) have been followed by a decline in the growth of their exports, though they differ from the British in that most of their pre-agreement rates of growth to these 13 countries were unsustainably high.

These results throw serious doubt on CBI and business claims that ceding responsibility for trade agreements to the EC has benefited UK exports. None of their submissions to the government make comparisons with the trade agreements of any independent countries, and are empty assertions of a kind that would be dismissed scathingly, or perhaps as a joke, by the marketing departments of every CBI member firm.

Both OECD and UN Comtrade data show that, by surrendering the right to conduct its own trade negotiations, the UK has sacrificed many years of freer trade for its exporters of both goods and services. An attempt is made to rough count the still-mounting value of these lost years of freer trade by supposing that an independent UK negotiating its own agreements had kept pace with Switzerland or Singapore. Any attempt to calculate the benefits of the Single Market should also include these substantial and continuing losses.

The second part of the investigation tries to answer the question that the minister raised but failed to answer satisfactorily: what would have happened if the Single Market programme had never been created? It does this by extending the exponential trendlines of the growth of exports of goods over the Common Market years 1973-1992 through the Single Market years 1993-2012. When these exponential trendlines are compared with the real rate of the growth of exports over these same two decades of the Single Market, they show that:

- Exports of goods of the 12 founder members of the Single Market to each other have been 14.6 per cent lower than they would have been had they continued to grow exactly as they had done under the Common Market, and are therefore nowhere near the minister's doubling claim.

- UK exports of goods to the other 11 founder members have been 22.3 per cent lower, while to other OECD countries only 10.9 per cent lower.

- Exports of non-member OECD countries to the EU were just 2.05 per cent lower, and have therefore performed almost as well as they did in the Common Market years.

- Thus the UK's exports have grown and benefited least during the Single Market, while those of non-member OECD countries have grown and benefited most.

- There is no evidence that the Single Market programme has helped the exports of the UK or other founder member countries to other OECD countries.

If the analysis is taken only to the eve of the financial crisis of 2008, both EU members as a whole and the UK alone perform rather better, though still not as well as in the Common Market decades, and only the exports of non-member countries to the EU exceed their growth during the Common Market decades. Hence the paradox of the Single Market: in terms of the growth of exports of goods, non-member countries have been its main beneficiaries, and still more paradoxically, those non-members that have not had any trade agreements with the EU – Australia, Canada, Japan and the United States – have benefited more than those that have: Turkey, Iceland, Norway and Switzerland.

Data on services exports is limited and uneven. The EC's preferred measure of integration of the Single Market – the proportions of intra and extra-EU exports as a percentage of GDP – shows that the degree of integration is extremely low, and has been sinking slowly but continuously since 2007, despite the repeated calls of successive British prime ministers that it be extended. Over the years 2002-2012, the extra-EU exports of services of 11 of the 12 founder members, and in particular those of the UK, have grown faster than their intra-EU exports. France is the sole exception.

These figures throw doubt on the very existence of an EU single market in services, which is distinguished from other markets by providing greater opportunities for trade amongst its members. To find out whether membership of the EU confers any advantage in services trade, the growth rates of the services exports of 20 member countries to other EU members between 2004 and 2012 were compared with those of 19 non-member countries. There is no statistically significant difference between them. By this measure, therefore, the advantages of members and the disadvantages of non-members in the 'single market' in services are both illusions. Indeed, given that non-member countries pay nothing for exporting to the

Single Market, other than the tariff and trade costs of individual exporters, they might reasonably be said to have benefited more from it than its own member countries.

These findings, along with evidence that Single Market members have suffered from distinctively high and severe unemployment compared with independent OECD countries, that their GDP and productivity have grown more slowly, and that the exports of 15 non-member countries to the rest of the EU have grown more rapidly than those of the UK, demonstrate that the image of the Single Market as the 'crown jewel' of the EU which has delivered 'substantial economic benefits' to the UK is a myth.

This myth seems to have originated in the efforts of the political elite of the early 1970s to convince the British people that entering the Common Market was in their best economic interest. In their attempts to persuade the British people that membership is in their interest, later governments have allowed this myth to survive and flourish by declining to provide regular, reliable and trustworthy measures and analyses of the costs and benefits of the Single Market which would have enabled British voters to assess for themselves the merits of the EU which their taxes support, and to which their government is now subject. This has led to the mis-selling over many years of the Single Market as a benefit to UK trade which, in scale and significance, dwarfs payment protection insurance (PPI), the only comparable contemporary case of selling illusory benefits at exorbitant cost. Many of the former political leaders who declined to collect reliable evidence when in office – Sir John Major, Kenneth Clarke, Tony Blair, Lord Mandelson – now play a leading part in the campaign for the UK to remain a member of the EU.

There is therefore a strong case for an independent, adequately-funded research and audit agency, similar to that of the Office for Budget Responsibility, the Office for National Statistics or the House of Commons Library, to examine the economic costs and benefits of the Single Market impartially, explain or resolve the paradox that non-members have been its main beneficiaries, and allow it to become a topic of normal, evidence-based political debate. It might well follow the advice and 'binding guidance' set out in the Green and Magenta books on evidence-based policy-making published by HM Treasury, which have hitherto never been applied to the EU project.

This investigation concludes by listing a few of the priority research topics this agency might address and notes the benefits it would have, for europhiles and eurosceptics alike. It would help to make the EC more accountable and the British electorate better informed, especially when it is asked to decide in a referendum whether the UK should continue as a member of the EU. But the case for such an agency remains as strong, whatever the outcome of the referendum might be.

# Part One

## The Myth of the Single Market's Trade Benefits

# 1

# A doubling of trade?
# A minister's claim
# to parliament

In written evidence submitted to the House of Lords Select Committee on the European Union in October 2010, the minister co-ordinating European matters for the Department for Business, Innovation and Skills (BIS), Ed Davey, claimed:

> Economic evidence shows that the Single Market has delivered substantial economic benefits. EU countries trade twice as much with each other as they would do in the absence of the Single Market programme. Given that, according to the OECD, a 10 percentage point increase in trade exposure is associated with a four per cent rise in income per capita, increased trade in Europe since the early 1980s may be responsible for around six per cent higher income per capita in the UK.[1]

Nine subsequent pages of this written evidence went on to say that there was 'scope for further gains' from the Single Market, for 'verifying that the regulatory framework was up to date', and for 'addressing bottlenecks on a comprehensive and coherent way'. Specifically, it mentioned 'more effective enforcement', and 'faster and cheaper dispute resolution procedures' and looked forward to the proposed services directive which it thought would release 'the untapped potential' of intra-EU trade in the services sector. Throughout, the tone was confident, optimistic, bullish, as if the Single Market was a well-designed engine needing some fine tuning to obtain its best performance.

My examination of OECD data on UK exports to EU members since 1973 had left a different impression. One simple measure is the share of UK goods exports to OECD countries going to the 12 founder members of the Single Market, but this was virtually the same in 2012 as it was in 1993, and slightly less than in 1973. This did not suggest that it had helped UK exporters in a significant way, especially as the share going to the three European countries that had not joined but merely entered trade agreements of one sort or another with the EU (Iceland, Norway and Switzerland), had doubled over the same period.[2] Odd as it may seem, the growth in the value of UK goods exports to other members has steadily *declined* as the UK entered into a closer relationship with the EU. They had grown by 137 per cent in real terms over the 13 years before Britain joined (1960-1972), by 171 per cent over the 20 years of the Common Market (1973-1992), but by just 81 per cent over the first 19 years of the Single Market (up to 2011).[3]

The contrast between the Common Market and Single Market decades is particularly dismal and well-documented. During the Common Market, UK goods exports to other EU members grew more rapidly than those of Australia, Argentina, Canada, Switzerland, Norway, New Zealand, South Africa and the United States, while during the Single Market their growth was slower than every single one of them. The US was an especially telling illustration of the difference between the two eras. Over the 20 years of the Common Market, UK exports to EU members grew faster than American exports, and by 1992 were 50 per cent higher in value. Thereafter, from the very first year of the Single Market, the differential between the two countries steadily declined, so that by 2011, for the first time since 1972, the value of US exports of goods to the EU exceeded the value of UK exports.[4] Other evidence pointed in the same direction. Over the years 1993 to 2011, the first 19 years of the Single Market, exports of goods from 27 non-member countries to EU members have grown at a faster rate than those of the UK and over the 11 years for which we have reasonable data, the services exports of 21 non-members have also done so.[5] Such figures leave one wondering not about the advantages of membership but about those of non-membership.

Evidence of this kind had left an impression of the Single Market not as a machine that needed fine tuning, but one with some fundamental design flaw that its enthusiastic salesmen were not too keen to mention. Rather than fine tuning, it seemed to require stripping down, along with a careful re-examination of the original drawings to work out why it had, for the UK at least, failed to perform as expected.

Coming across the minister's claim that the Single Market had 'delivered substantial economic benefits' that 'EU countries trade twice as much with each other as they would do in the absence of the Single Market programme' naturally prompted a serious re-think. Where were the substantial economic benefits that had never been previously identified and measured? Or was it that the available evidence referred only to exports, and that its 'substantial economic benefits' were of some other kind? Maybe there were other sources of evidence known only to the minister and to BIS? There was only one way these questions could be answered. I submitted a freedom of information (FOI) request to BIS asking for the evidence on which the minister's claim to the House of Lords sub-committee was based.

## Why pursue this particular claim?

While waiting for a reply, a number of other questions came to me, the first one being: 'Why bother?' Claims are made every other day about the benefits of the EU, so why make a fuss about this particular one? In the House of Commons debate after his use of Britain's veto in 2012, David Cameron had claimed that the EU was good for trade, investment and jobs and every member in the ensuing debate appeared to take it for granted that this claim was true. He hadn't given any evidence, and no one was impolite enough to ask him what evidence he had in mind. But then his claim was bland enough to be taken as an acceptable rhetorical flourish in a speech about his actions in Brussels the day before, rather than a report of the findings of a government inquiry. Why not treat Ed Davey's claim in the same spirit, as an exuberant rhetorical flourish intended to give his testimony to the House of Lords an upbeat introduction? Besides, a lot of water has flown under the bridge since 2010. Why not let the matter rest?

For several reasons, I did not leave it to rest. This occasion was rather different. It was a written submission, and therefore more considered than a figure of speech, and its formulation implied that it had been the subject of careful statistical analysis. Moreover, while debates in the Commons cannot be cluttered with detailed statistical evidence, this was an occasion where such claims might, and indeed were, expected to be the subject of close and extended scrutiny by well-informed interrogators. If this statement is not questioned in that setting, then where or when will it be? No members of the committee had questioned this claim, so it had already been granted some kind of validation, and was already on its way to be taken as the truth, as part of the conventional wisdom. It was also catchy enough to be quoted on any suitable moment to clinch an argument. For all these reasons, it seemed worth bothering about.

Other reasons persuaded me not to let the matter rest. Having read some of BIS's research reports on other subjects, I had formed a favourable impression of the quality of their research work, especially when compared with that of the Treasury. If telling, comprehensive and reliable evidence about the 'substantial economic benefits' of the Single Market existed they would, I felt sure, certainly know about it and have no reason not to direct me to it. They might even have conducted it themselves. Or some of their research staff may have been seconded to the EC, and brought back useful data. An FOI request might give me the first public sight of some hitherto unpublished valuable data.

While waiting for a reply, some phrases in the short paragraph raised other questions about the nature of the evidence that might be offered to support the minister's claim. Overall, his statement conveyed the impression that 'substantial economic benefits' had been delivered to the UK, but on closer reading the statement did not exactly say that. It only said that the Single Market had delivered substantial economic benefits, but not to whom. So it might be that they had been delivered to the EU as a whole, while the UK had not shared them, and this might be why they were difficult to find.

Likewise, the dates mentioned raised questions. At first glance, it appears to be a claim about the Single Market, but it then refers to EU countries' trade with each other without any dates, and then to support the claim about the increase in trade since the early 1980s, long before the Single Market had come into existence or even been agreed to, so it was unclear when the doubling of trade among members of the Single Market was supposed to have occurred.

The arithmetic of the figures mentioned raised further questions. The Organisation for Economic Cooperation and Development (OECD) suggested that a 10 per cent rise in trade exposure led to a four per cent increase in income per capita. But the minister claimed that trade had not increased by 10 per cent, but by 100 per cent, which following the OECD argument would presumably have led to a very large increase in income per head. Instead, they only claimed that the Single Market *may* have been responsible for higher income per capita in the UK of around just six per cent. Or of course it may not, so there is the possibility that nothing at all was being claimed for the UK.

As I waited for a response, the argument therefore began to seem rather ambiguous, fuzzy, and with acres of wriggle room, but in the end the first reading seemed the reasonable and likely meaning of the minister's text: the Single Market programme had delivered substantial economic benefits to the UK and other members; and the UK, along with other member countries, traded twice as much with each other as they would have done in the absence of it.

This is how the members of the House of Lords select committee seem to have read and accepted it, before moving on to consider the questions they had put to the BIS. They did not ask how and where this evidence was collected, nor have any questions about whether the benefits were evenly distributed across the EU, or why a doubling of trade could only mean a six per cent increase in income. They all appear to have calmly taken for granted what seemed to me a staggering achievement, and then moved on to rather amiable questions to the minister about how to build on success, the government's priorities in the future development of the Single Market, and certain operational details.

## A disappointing and disconcerting reply

The BIS reply (reprinted as Appendix A) prompted mixed feelings: some disappointment, then surprise, and finally, after time spent studying the sources to which they referred, dismay and disbelief.

The immediate disappointment was that there had been no need for an FOI request, since the evidence on which they had relied was already in the public domain. There was no hidden and unpublished cache of data collected by BIS to analyse and discuss. No scoop after all!

The surprise was provoked by the dates of two main sources to which they referred. The first, to justify the claims about the economic benefits of the Single Market, was a fairly well-known report authored by four members of the staff of the EC's Directorate General for Economic and Financial Affairs (DGECFIN) published in 2007.[6] The second source related directly to the claim that 'EU countries trade twice as much with each other as they would do in the absence of the Single Market programme' was an article by three French professors in the Canadian Journal of Economics, published in 2005.[7]

The dates of these publications made it clear that the minister was not relying on recent evidence in his statement to the select committee, presumably because he did not have any from his own department to give. Given that evidence analysed in reports usually precedes publication dates by a few years, his oral testimony in January 2011 was therefore probably going to rest on evidence that had been collected, at the very latest in 2007 and more probably several years earlier. Could it be that one of the two main departments responsible for UK policy towards the EU had no more up-to-date evidence to present to parliament than that which had been collected three, four or five years earlier? The surprise started to turn into disbelief.

The disbelief grew stronger when I thought about the sources of the data to which I had been referred. There is no reason of course why first-rate, authoritative evidence should not come either from EC staff in Brussels or from three professors in Paris, though it seemed unlikely that they could have quite the same interest in the impact on the UK economy, as local British studies might have done. What was more difficult to believe was that a minister of the UK government reporting to parliament about the Single Market had no current evidence of its merits generated from within his own department, or apparently from any other Whitehall department.

The paper by the EC staff raised more concern, for though it was written by four members of DGECFIN, a further 12 were credited for their inputs and it must therefore have been close to presenting the consensus view of the EC. Nothing wrong with that of course, though it is not altogether inconceivable that they might have their own agenda, and be less than impartial in their analysis of the benefits of the Single Market. Moreover, in the interests of EU solidarity, the EC often seems reluctant either in its predictions or analyses, to distinguish winners and losers among member countries, so it seemed unlikely that it would learn much about which of them the UK might have been.

The absence of complementary UK sources was also vaguely unsettling on another ground. There is a view that national governments are one of the means by which the EC itself is scrutinised and held to account, and it was therefore disconcerting to discover that a UK government minister, accounting to parliament for government policy towards the EU, relied on evidence provided by the EC itself. Something seemed amiss about that, almost as if the UK government already saw itself as a department subordinate to the EC. All these misgivings were, however, quickly put aside, since the more immediate issue was to decide whether, and where, the two primary sources mentioned in the BIS reply provided evidence to support the minister's claim.

# 2

# Reviewing the evidence

First of all, it must be said, the study in the *Canadian Journal of Economics* does not make any attempt to see how far the Single Market has increased trade between member countries, or what it might have been in its absence. It does not contain the phrase that EU countries, 'trade twice as much with each other as they would do in the absence of the Single Market programme' or anything like it. Its authors, Lionel Fontagne, Thierry Mayer and Soledad Zignago, address a quite distinct issue that has long concerned analysts of international trade, the so-called 'border effect puzzle'. That is, why trade within a country is greater than trade across its national borders. The specific border effects with which Fontagne, Mayer and Zignago are concerned are those affecting trade within 'the triad' of the EU, Japan and the US.

To measure how various factors that are known to contribute to the border effect might have impacted on the triad, the authors created a model. They devised proxies for tariffs and non-tariff barriers (NTBs), for the home bias of consumers, for product differentiation and for levels of foreign direct investment (FDI), since this last may be a substitute for trade across borders. They also endeavoured to take account of the impact of language and distance (for which they created their own database), both of which separate the three members of the triad and are known to affect the volume of trade. They then fed this data into their model, along with data for the years 1976-1999 from the trade and protection database of the World Bank. The 1999 date confirmed my fears about dated evidence.

Their most relevant finding in the present context was that the border effects of trade amongst member countries of the EU are lower than the border effects of trade between other members of the triad, and that all the border effects for intra-EU trade 'are regularly decreasing over time'.[1] They therefore concluded that 'the European integration revealed by this decrease in border effects is an on-going and successful process'.[2] However, they also found that the ease of access in one of the other trade relationships in the triad came close to that of EU member countries to each other, namely that of US exports to Japan. Japan, they concluded, 'would seem almost as open to US exports as German consumers are to French exporters'. This 'spectacular result' clearly took them a little by surprise, and led them to wonder whether their equations and proxies had correctly estimated for the effect of distance on trade between the two countries.

More generally, their results pointed to 'important differences and asymmetries in the quality of market access'. A typical European country in the late 1990s has an average ratio of trade with self over trade with another EU country around 13 times larger than that predicted by the model, which gives, they think, an idea of the substantial level of fragmentation remaining in the EU.[3] The same ratio for the US exports to Japan is 16.8 while that for flows in the reverse direction is 23.8 and that for EU exports to the US is 32.5. They went on to give a detailed breakdown to show the variations by industrial sectors. In the end, they not unreasonably claim:

> ...the level of border effects in a given industry can be caused by actual protection set by governments (tariffs and NTBs), home-biased preferences of consumers, and the degree of homogeneity of the good traded. The set of proxies used in our regressions to capture those determinants explains a substantial part of border effects. The explanatory power of those variables ranges from 32.3 per cent of the Japan to EU border effect, to 45.7 per cent of the Japan to United States one. While the border effect puzzle is not totally solved, our theory-consistent method coupled with standard economic explanations manage to provide a good overall picture of the causes of market access difficulties in the triad.

Nothing in this study, as far as I can discover, shows what the increase of trade between EU member countries might have been 'in the absence of the Single Market programme.' Perhaps with some re-working of the model, it might, I guess, have yielded evidence by examining the amount of trade when intra-EU border effects were higher than they have been since 1993, but no attempt is made to do this. If BIS researchers themselves had done something along these lines, they would, I imagine, have been pleased to draw it to my attention. As published, however, the only support it provides for the minister's claim is that intra-EU border effects are indeed lower than elsewhere in the triad. However, the example of American exports to Japan raises awkward questions, since it showed how border effects might be reduced, in the absence of any sort of Single Market programme, and in some products in some years, to an even lower level than those of the EU countries to each other. Sensibly perhaps, the minister and his advisers ignored those kind of details.

At the end of it all, one is left wondering why BIS would want to observe the benefits on intra-EU trade looking back to the years 1976-1999 through a prism invented by three clever researchers testing their border effects model, when current data about that trade can be observed directly – in broad daylight, so to speak – by looking at United Nations, World Trade Organisation or OECD databases.

## A European Commission report
## on the eve of the crisis

The second source to which BIS referred me, the EC report of 2007, looked much more promising.[4] The abstract observes that 'the internal market... has been the source of large macro-economic benefits'. The authors say that the second of its three parts 'puts together a comprehensive body of empirical evidence, based on the analysis of trade, FDI, mergers and acquisitions (M&A), prices and regulation data, which allows for a thorough stock taking exercise of what has been achieved in terms of European economic integration'. These words suggested that this was the perfect place to find evidence to support the minister's claim.

On further examination, it seems a little less than perfect. 'Thorough stock taking exercise' does not seem to be an altogether accurate description of it, since it is concerned not only with what has happened, but also with what should have happened, what was expected to happen, and what might yet happen. Indeed, it often seems to be an extended springboard for the third part of the report which outlines the 'Steps towards a deeper economic integration'. It would also have been a little more reassuring, simply as a stocktaking, if it had included some assessments of the costs of integration for member countries, but none are mentioned. It would have been still more reassuring if the question of whether or not there should be further integration had been left open until it was finished, when they, and the reader, might have been able to consider whether more integration was an appropriate response.

That said, there is no lack of evidence and of candid, blunt, impartial assessments that one expects to find in any good stocktaking, so it deserves careful reading. In contrast to the words of the abstract (which one suspects may have been written by someone else), the authors say their results show 'somewhat of a mixed picture', which includes many dashed hopes and unfulfilled expectations. Even if these were only included to show 'how the potential of the internal market has… not yet been fully exploited', and to make the case for more integration in the third part of the report, their candour and the absence of window-dressing in most sections is welcome, commendable and rather unexpected.

This report is especially worthy of close attention because it traces the impact of the Single Market almost to the brink of the financial crisis starting in 2007/8, and to its own high-water mark, one might say. It therefore portrays the Single Market as it was supposed to work, before it was rocked by sovereign debt crises. Moreover, since so many DGECOFIN staff members contributed to it, one may assume it catches the EC consensus at that high point. It is therefore a historical document of some importance. For that reason, a brief summary of its conclusions can be found at Appendix B; I have listed some of the most salient points in Box A.

## Did the EC report support the minister's claim?

This EC report is in its own way a remarkable document, especially to British eyes long accustomed to hearing from their political leaders that the Single Market is some prized asset that the British people must, on no account, let slip from their grasp. Here in sharp

**Box A:** Problems of the Single Market: excerpts from a 2007 EC report

**Excerpts from the European Commission report** *Steps towards a deeper economic integration: the Internal Market in the 21st century*

'There has been a slowdown of trade growth within the EU15 and euro-zone relative to trade growth with third partners'

'The trade boosting effect of the introduction of the euro has... been far less pronounced than the trade effect of enlargement.'

'...since 2000 the trade effect of the enlargement process and particularly intra-EU15 trade integration, seem to have stalled.'

'EU product markets remain heavily regulated, business dynamism is insufficient and prices rigidities are persistent.'

'...the share of extra EU suppliers in... consumption... has gradually increased at the expense of domestic production.'

'Not only are EU firms less active in fast growing markets but also they have not managed to improve their performance in fast growing sectors at world level although this was one of the main goals of the 1992 Single Market programme.'

'...the Internal Market... has not led to a sufficient shift of the specialisation of the production sector towards the more technology intensive sectors where EU competitiveness can be more sustainable in the long-run.'

'16.6 per cent of world exports of low technology goods originated in the EU25 while only 8.4 per cent and 1.6 per cent came from the US and Japan. Furthermore, the EU25 reveals a comparative disadvantage in high technology sectors including ICT 52...'

'The Internal Market does not seem to have been a sufficient catalyst for innovation and resource reallocation towards technology intensive activities.'

'...the innovative performance of the EU as a whole and of most EU countries lags significantly behind that of top performers such as the US and Japan... What is more worrying is the widening gap between the laggards and front-runners and between the EU and other developed economies.'

'Since 2001 the volume of FDI from the rest of the world into the EU25 has gradually declined.'

'...the Internal Market has not been able to deliver in terms of promoting further the role of the EU with respect to global investment flows.'

'The internal market two-fold objective of making the EU a more attractive place for foreign investors and of boosting the presence and competitive position of EU firms in world markets seems far from being achieved.'

'The Internal Market is also losing its attractiveness for international R&D investment. Multinational companies prefer to carry out their R&D activities in the US – and more recently in China and India – rather than in the EU.'

Source: Fabienne Ilzkovitz, Adriaan Dierx, Viktoria Kovacs and Nuno Sousa, European Economy, Economic Papers, N° 271 January 2007, *Steps towards a deeper economic integration: the Internal Market in the 21st century, A contribution to the Single Market Review.* European Commission, Directorate-General For Economic and Financial Affairs, ISSN 1725-3187, http://ec.europa.eu/economy_finance/index_en.htm

contrast we read, even before the financial crisis, of a succession of policy failures. Perhaps the most striking of them, from a British point of view, is that 'there is little difference between trade (in services) between EU25 member states and trade between the EU and third countries'.[5] In other words, after 12 years of the Single Market during which successive British prime ministers had been urging and promising that the Single Market would be extended to services, there was still barely any difference in the trade in services between members and non-members. This is surely a most remarkable fact. We will return to it later.

But our present purpose is to find within this document the 'substantial economic benefits' that the minister claimed had been delivered by the Single Market. One may immediately drop from further consideration FDI and innovation, which are explicitly recognised by the authors as Single Market failures. As we continue the search, we must also recognise that what the authors take to be an economic benefit may not be recognised as such by outside observers. The authors' main focus is on the integration of the member economies, and hence their frequent comparisons with the US, which they take as the model of what an integrated single market should look like. Thus, any change in any of their indices of integration, or what they take to be indices of integration, such as price convergence and M&A, is from their point of view an economic benefit, though it is unlikely to be widely viewed as such.

We should also recognise the fiendishly difficult problem, which the authors intermittently acknowledge, of distinguishing the impact of the Single Market from the impact of the euro, of enlargement, and of contemporaneous technological, demographic and economic changes. The euro is clearly in their sights, but that of enlargement is particularly problematic, since the collapse of communism and the sudden emergence of many new capitalist markets would, one imagines, have affected FDI, M&A and employment in EU countries, even if none of these countries had elected to become members of the EU.

On the grounds that some of the micro-economic changes examined, such as M&A activity, instability of market leadership, entry and exit rates and price convergence, cannot be unambiguously defined either as benefits or as consequences of the Single Market or both, I will also exclude them from further consideration. All these micro-economic changes might better be seen as changes which economic theory suggests will, over the long-run, yield 'substantial economic benefits' to the inhabitants of the EU. They are theoretically, and perhaps reasonably, anticipated economic benefits, but not yet, as far as we can tell, delivered ones.[6]

When therefore we look for 'substantial economic benefits' that have been delivered, we are left with their evidence on trade and employment, as well as the estimated increase in EU GDP of 2.2 per cent. Trade and employment are commonly among the first things to be mentioned by those who favour UK membership of the EU. As noted earlier, the prime minister referred to both in his speech to the House of Commons. If the report provided evidence of significant improvements in one or both, either for the EU generally or for the UK in particular, then Ed Davey's remark about 'substantial economic benefits' might have been justified.

The report provides no such evidence on either count. On the contrary, as we have seen, the report refers to the slowdown of intra-EU trade growth that had begun 10 years before the minister appeared before the select committee, and it frankly admits the failure of member countries to meet the 1992 goals of the Single Market programme by improving their performance in fast-growing sectors of world trade. There is no evidence to suggest that the Single Market brought any 'substantial economic benefits' in trade, and nothing at all to suggest that EU countries 'trade twice as much with each other as they would do in the absence of the Single Market programme'.

What then of employment? Given the report's conclusion that 'the enlarged internal market... is an important source of growth and jobs', the minister would appear to be on firmer ground. However, it is not that firm, and well short of rock solid, since that conclusion was based on an estimate from a model, and is preceded by 'a word of caution' about the multiple simulations and assumptions of the model from which its estimate of an increase in the level of employment in the Single Market was derived. We therefore have to keep our fingers crossed that the model has correctly allowed for all the other factors that might affect the level of employment, and has given a reliable estimate that the internal market was responsible for an increase of 1.5 per cent in the level of employment. The authors conclude with the comment that 'employment levels have increased significantly'. But how would they know whether this increase is significant or not without comparative evidence? They did not conduct any comparative research on this point and so we will try to make good its absence and see whether the estimated increase in employment is significant or not.

Since we do not have access to the Quest model the EC uses for macroeconomic policy analysis, we will simply look at the increases in the gross level of employment over the years in question, 1996 to 2002. The OECD database on the civilian labour force shows that over those years, the labour force of the 15 members of the Single Market increased by 10.91 per cent. The EC report included the new member countries in their calculations, and therefore drew conclusions about EU25, but since none of them had joined the EU until 2004, which is beyond the years under examination, it is not clear how they did this, or indeed whether they should have done so. We have therefore ignored the post-2004 entrants. By comparison with the EU15, the civilian labour force of all the other non-EU OECD countries increased, over the same years, by 10.81 per cent, that is to say a difference of 0.10 per cent less than the increase in the EU15, a difference which is probably within the margin of error of collection of these statistics.

What should we conclude? That the Single Market contributed the 1.75 per cent the report mentioned to the level of employment in member countries? That without it, the EU member countries would have increased their employment not by 10.91 per cent but by only 9.16 per cent? Probably not, since statistics for level of employment and civilian labour force are compiled in different ways. It therefore seems safer to conclude that the civilian labour forces of the EU15 increased at roughly the same rate as all other OECD countries, and that the Single Market programme had no identifiable, differentiating impact on the level of employment at all.

Further comparisons do not provide much help to gauge the scale of the Single Market achievement. The three European OECD countries that declined to join the EU, Iceland, Norway and Switzerland, increased their civilian labour force by 9.31 per cent, slightly less therefore than the full members of the Single Market, while the US increased its labour force significantly more, by 13.05 per cent. This would presumably reassure the EC research team, given that the US is their favoured model of integration. The UK increased least of all, by 8.66 per cent.

All these figures about the increase in employment are, however, a little beside the point. The number one index of the success of any economic policy in every modern democracy is the level or rate of unemployment, not the level of employment. Indeed, the omission of this index in what is presented as 'a thorough stock taking of what has been achieved in terms of European economic integration' is the one serious black mark against the entire exercise.[7]

The full, calamitous record of the unemployment of the 12 founder members of the Single Market over 21 years is reproduced in Burrage, 'A Club of High and Severe Unemployment' (London: Civitas, 2015). It shows that, since the start of the Single Market, its 12 founder members have had a distinctively high rate of both unemployment and of long-term unemployment, when compared with 10 independent mainly OECD countries, and most especially when compared with non-member European economies, Switzerland, Norway and Iceland.

Media attention was drawn to the severity of this problem when the post-crisis levels of unemployment in southern Europe, and especially of youth unemployment, reached previously unimaginable levels after the financial crisis. However, high unemployment has been a distinguishing characteristic of the Single Market throughout the entire life of the programme. Its members can fairly be described as a club of high and severe unemployment. It is a shameful record, particularly as continental Europeans are inclined to think their social model is rather superior to that of other countries, especially 'Anglo-Saxon' countries, which are less caring towards the welfare of their citizens. If it is a grievous omission of the EC staff report to overlook these facts, then for a minister to airily observe that the Single Market had delivered 'substantial economic benefits', and then to refer only incidentally to the appalling problem of youth unemployment in some member countries, is scarcely less so.[8]

| Table 1: GDP Growth of EU25, 2002–2006 | | | | | |
|---|---|---|---|---|---|
| GDP Growth | 2002 | 2003 | 2004 | 2005 | 2006 |
| EC estimate of the internal market's 'total GDP effect' on EU25 % | 1.96 | 2.05 | 2.08 | 2.15 | 2.18 |
| EC estimate of the internal market's 'total GDP effect' in €billions | 189.2 | 198.7 | 206.2 | 215.4 | 222.6 |
| World Bank reported annual per cent GDP growth of EU25 | 1.31 | 1.48 | 2.52 | 2.06 | 3.42 |

*EC estimates and World Bank data.
Source: p.57, Ilzkovitz, *op.cit*. http://data.worldbank.org/indicator: GDP growth (annual %)

The gains in GDP from the internal market estimated by the Quest model rise from 1.96 per cent (or €189.2bn) in 2002 to 2.18 per cent (or €222.6 bn) in 2006. There are certain things to be said about this estimate.[9] First, it includes both the impact of the liberalisation of network industries, and enlargement, as 'GDP effects of the internal market'. While inclusion of the former is reasonable, inclusion of the latter seems rather questionable if the aim is to discover GDP gains of the internal market. Second, the estimated gains are difficult to square with the World Bank record of the annual percentage growth of the EU's GDP over these same years, which are shown alongside the EC estimate in Table 1.[10]

If the commission estimates were correct, then the internal market contribution to the EU's GDP sometimes exceeded the actual recorded growth of GDP, which means that without the internal market the EU's GDP would actually have fallen in these years, and in the other years achieved an unusually low rate of growth, neither of which unlikely possibilities does the EC team stop to explain.

Third, there is no means of checking how realistic and accurate were the various simulations, assumptions, and subordinate estimates on which these estimates were based, since the track record of the Quest model has not been publicly assessed as far as I know.

However, for the sake of argument we will put these reservations on one side, and address the claim that the EC authors are making that the internal market is responsible for an increase of €223bn in the GDP of member countries. This seems like a very large sum.

One way in which we can judge just how large it might be is to compare it with the EC's own estimate of the 'administrative costs' in member countries, meaning those 'incurred in meeting reporting requirements' which were given in its strategic reviews of the Better Regulation programme launched in co-operation with OECD. In 2006, for example, its website claimed that these costs might be reduced by a quarter and then estimated the 'economic benefits from such action... at an increase in the level of GDP of up to 1.5 per cent of GDP or up to €150bn'.[11] If 25 per cent of the administrative costs then amounted to €150bn and about 1.5 per cent of GDP, it is reasonable to infer that the EU's estimate of total administrative costs were 'up to' €600bn per annum and 'up to' six per cent of the EU's GDP.[12] Suddenly €223bn seems quite a modest sum, and a 2.2 per cent gain in GDP for a six per cent outlay per annum cost looks like a rather poor deal.

Another way of getting some sense of the scale of the Single Market's contribution to the growth of the EU's GDP is to compare its growth with that of other similar but independent economies. In Appendix D, it is compared with 10 independent OECD economies, with a separate analysis of the three countries that are the EU's nearest neighbours in Europe.[13]

The GDP growth of the EU over the 21 years of the Single Market has been relatively slow. Over the two decades from 1993 to 2012, the GDP of the 10 independent countries grew by 54 per cent, and the three independent European countries on their own by 46 per cent, while that of the 12 founder members of the Single Market grew by 38 per cent. If we measure only to 2006, which is the point at which the Quest model estimated a gain of 2.2 per cent attributable to the Single Market, the 10 independent countries had grown by 45 per cent, the three European independent countries by 35 per cent and the EU by 37 per cent. By that year therefore, the EU had grown rather more, 1.57 per cent more to be precise, than the three independent European countries, but 8 per cent less than the other OECD countries.

Alas, this slight edge was lost in the crisis and post crisis years. By 2013 the GDP of the 10 independent countries had grown by 19 per cent more than that of the EU members, and the three independent European countries by 10 per cent more. Is €223bn still a large sum? If the EU had grown at the same rate as the 10 independents by 2013 - by 57 per cent instead of 28 per cent – its total GDP in 2013 would have been $5.2tn instead of $3.5tn, meaning that it would have additionally increased by the same amount as Italy's total GDP in 2013, which was just under $1.7tn. And if its GDP had grown by 38 per cent like the three independent European countries, its GDP in 2013 would have been $886bn larger, which is more than the combined GDPs of the Netherlands and Ireland, which in 2013 together totalled $882bn. Suddenly, the estimated increase of €223bn attributable to the Single Market by 2006 seems a rather small sum.

The EC estimate of the Single Market's 2.2 per cent and €223bn contribution to the EU's GDP over some 13 years was presented without reference to the GDP growth of other countries, and therefore gave no means of judging how significant it might have been. Isolating figures in this manner was presumably meant to impress, persuade and convince, and it may well have done so. However, comparative evidence raises the more difficult, and much more important, question of why the Single Market programme has done little to prevent the GDP of the EU growing at a significantly slower rate than that of comparable independent countries.

It might be, of course, that the Single Market was indeed a benefit to its members, and that without it, the EU's GDP would have been 2.2 per cent less than it actually was. Somehow, it seems rather perverse to count this as a 'significant economic benefit' to help the minister's case. The Single Market was intended to improve the EU's efficiency and competitiveness, and therefore the growth of its GDP. Despite its help over two decades, and its costs, the growth of the EU's GDP has failed to keep pace with independent countries (discussed further in Appendix D). It would take more than a little *chutzpah* to then claim it was nonetheless a significant economic benefit because its GDP might, for some unexplained reason, have grown at an even slower pace.

# Were the minister's claims justified?

Having patiently examined all the sources to which BIS referred me, including those that Ed Davey could have consulted before his statement, and the later ones that he could not have done, it is now possible to say whether or not the minister's evidence drew fairly and reasonably on the research data available to him when he presented evidence to the select committee in October 2010 and then appeared before it in January 2011.[14]

He was entitled to mention a few possible benefits; that is, benefits which economic theory reasonably leads us to expect some time in the future rather than already delivered and documented benefits. For instance, border effects on goods exports within the Single Market continued to decline up to the year 1999 – some 11 years before his evidence - and they were markedly lower than those on EU goods exported to Japan or the US, though not than those on US goods exported to Japan. The UK might therefore reasonably be said to have benefited from freer trade to fellow members of the EU. Likewise, the various micro-economic changes noted in the EC paper as indications of integration, such as M&A activity, price convergence, the instability of market leadership, and the sectoral diversification of market leaders might reasonably be expected to yield economic benefits in terms of competition and productivity at some point, over the long run, though there was no evidence that these benefits were entirely due to the Single Market, or that any had, thus far, actually been delivered.

If, however, he had any of these benefits in mind, he should surely also have added an explanation that they were uncertain, indirect and only likely to be observed at some time in the future. Most observers, however, would take it that his claim that the EU had 'delivered substantial economic benefits' referred to gains in trade and employment. But there is, as we have just seen, no evidence of either type of gain in any of these sources. None of them make the claim that there has been a doubling of the level of trade that might have been expected in the absence of the Single Market. That assertion is not to be found in them, and none of them present any evidence that would lead one to think that it is remotely near the truth. The EC report of 2007 noted that intra-EU trade had 'stalled' in recent years. That report was also the only source that referred to employment gains, but its cautious estimate of a possible gain in the level of employment was given without comparative data to enable anyone to assess its significance, and it wholly ignored the EU's distinctively high levels of unemployment, and of long-term unemployment.

Judging by the sources referenced by BIS, Ed Davey's knowledge of the impact of the Single Market was limited and dated. He could know nothing of what might have been the Single Market's benefits for the UK in trade or employment, whatever its benefits may have been for the EU as a whole, because none of the evidence on which he relied referred specifically to the UK. He altogether ignored the string of failures mentioned in the EC report. When he later gave oral testimony to the select committee in January 2011, he proceeded as if the Single Market was a success story, and we only had 'to make sure it was constantly modernised' and press to extend its digitalisation and its coverage of services.

If there is any defence for this, it is that the select committee members all seem to have wanted to believe that the Single Market was a successful and worthwhile project fulfilling most of the hopes that had been placed in it, even before his oral testimony began. Their questions were therefore not about the serious problems that the EC report had identified. Instead, they asked such questions as 'How should confidence in the Single Market be restored?' and 'Is the UK affected by market or integration fatigue?'[15] Their main concern seemed, in short, to be how the image of the Single Market might be burnished a little brighter and why many British people seemed stubbornly reluctant to recognise its benefits.[16]

In hindsight, this session of the select committee (sub-committee B) revealed little about the problems and consequences of the Single Market at the time. If anything, it demonstrated that the Single Market has been defined by firmly-held beliefs in the value of free trade, supplemented by impressions, hearsay and hopes, rather than by empirical research of its actual effects.

# A more accurate statement to parliament

We may demonstrate just how firmly-held beliefs may define experience of the Single Market, and just how far the minister strayed from an accurate answer, if we imagine for a moment that another minister had come to the committee in his place, depending on exactly the same sources of evidence available to the real minister, but without any decided views on the merits of the Single Market, and intending simply to report as accurately as he or she could on its impact thus far. This requires some guesswork of course, but it does enable us to illustrate how far the research cited to me by BIS would have taken this imaginary minister. Here are some excerpts from his or her introductory remarks and answers to the sub-committee's questions.

### Introductory remarks

As you are aware, ever since the UK joined the European Economic Community nearly 40 years ago, it has not been the policy of any UK government to regularly monitor the consequences of any programmes that the Community, and later the Union, or the Commission has chosen to adopt. The best evidence available to me about the Single Market is that collected by EC staff some three years ago.

Unfortunately, this only refers to the EU as a whole, so I can only infer the possible benefits to the UK by scaling down from the EU, which is not always a reliable procedure. Moreover, this EC report says nothing about the costs of the Single Market, so I can only give you estimates of its benefits, and have no way of knowing whether they outweigh the costs.

The benefits to trade appear to have stalled, and while the EC staff estimate that the level of employment has increased by 1.75 per cent during the programme, we are unable to say whether this is less or more than independent countries over the same period.

Unfortunately, the member countries have not attracted FDI as hoped, nor has the programme had any discernible impact on the rate of innovation.

Perhaps the best news is that the so-called 'border effects' on trade between members consistently declined in the early years of the programme up to 1999. We think this is due to the programme, and we also think that this has been increasing the competitiveness and efficiency of European businesses, this being one of the reasonably expected consequences of free trade.

There are a number of other micro-economic changes, such as price convergence in the early years of the programme that has now slowed down, increased sectoral concentration, greater instability of market leadership, increased cross-border mergers and cross-border marketing, changes in pricing strategies of firms including reductions in mark ups. All of these things indicate that the Single Market in goods is becoming more integrated, which should lead to a more competitive and efficient economy in the future, and therefore benefit the workers and consumers of the Single Market over the longer run.

### Does the current economic environment require a re-thinking of the Single Market?

One of the more surprising results reported by the EC staff was that while intra-EU trade has stalled, and failed to meet the targets of 1992 in various respects, imports from non-member countries have grown more rapidly.

While we naturally welcome the contribution our programme has made to world trade, we did not expect that its main beneficiaries would be countries that were not sitting around the table with us and helping to make the rules, or indeed paying any of the costs of the programme. So yes! Some re-thinking of the Single Market might be good idea, so that we might better understand how it works and why non-members appear to have benefited more than its own members.

**How should confidence in the Single Market be restored? Is the UK affected by market or integration fatigue?**

In the absence of reliable evidence, public opinion has had to rely on media reports which are often less than accurate. Members of the government, led by the prime minister, will continue, at every opportunity, to reassure the public of the benefits of EU membership. We can also, I think, rely on former prime ministers, chancellors and EU trade commissioners who have played a role in the construction of the EU project to add their authority and experience to this cause.

This may perhaps help to restore public confidence. However, in the absence of reliable and trustworthy evidence of the promised benefits in terms of trade and jobs, it is bound to be an uphill task. So yes, it might be that there is a certain amount of market or integration fatigue, which might more accurately be described as scepticism, amongst the public at large.

In 2007 – and this is the most recent evidence available to me – a group of senior EC staff were of the view that if integration is pursued more vigorously in the future there will be significant gains for the EU, especially in regard to trade in services, which the programme has so far hardly affected at all. We have trusted EC reports in the past, and have every hope that, this time around, things might turn out as they predict, and that the UK will share in those gains.

If the minister had said something along these lines, the subsequent interrogation and discussion might, one imagines, and hopes, have had a different tone and taken an altogether different direction than the amiable chatter about operational details that actually occurred. It might have prompted research which would have taken us a little closer to understanding the failures and problems of the Single Market, and perhaps helped to judge whether more integration was the solution. The wider public debate about UK membership of the EU might also have been a little more informed and reasonable than it currently is.

# Did BIS retrospectively vindicate the minister?

Although the two sources which BIS gave me to support the minister's remarks failed to do so, it also referred to two further sources of evidence, published after 2010. In the hope that they might provide some retrospective justification for his remarks, they were also examined for details of the significant economic benefits of the Single Market programme, and the doubling of trade between its members.

The first is the volume of papers which BIS itself published together with the Centre of Economic Policy Research (CEPR).[17] This seeks, according to the preface by the then secretary of state, Vince Cable, 'to draw together evidence about the impact that the Single Market has had to date and establish where the priorities should be going forward'. This description of the contents of the volume is so inaccurate and misleading that it makes one wonder if the secretary of state read it. Some of the contributors certainly discuss future priorities, but none of them draw together any 'evidence about the impact that the Single Market has had to date', nor do they even attempt to do so, or cite any sources that might have done so. There is little point here in reviewing these papers to substantiate the secretary of state's misleading assertion, since the volume contains a chapter-by-chapter summary of its content.

In the entire volume, there is only a single, solitary empirical proposition that might be said to cast some light on 'the impact that the Single Market has had to date'. To show 'the positive effect on the UK's trade with the new member states' as a result of the Single Market it reported, on three occasions, that UK exports 'to the EU12 have doubled since 2004'.[18] In this context, the EU12 refers to countries that have joined since 2004. Unfortunately, the volume gives no citation saying where the evidence for the doubling of exports to the EU12 is to be found. Nor does it distinguish between goods and services, or say whether the growth is real or nominal, or give any dates over which the doubling occurred, or name which of the new member countries it has in mind – a relevant consideration when trying to verify the claim since the EU12 countries have joined at different dates since 2004.

The OECD publishes a full set of data for the years 2004-2012 of UK exports to only three of the post-2004 entrants to the EU: the Czech Republic, Hungary and Poland. This shows that the UK has doubled the value of its exports to these new members since 2004, in real terms (in 2004 US$), by 99.47 per cent to be precise, in current value dollars by 143 per cent.

What the editors of the BIS volume did not point out was that 21 non-member countries increased their exports to these same three countries, over these same years, by more than 100 per cent, Canada in current value dollars by 242 per cent, Singapore by 331 per cent, Korea by nearly 500 per cent. How can an increase of 143 per cent be sensibly said to show 'the positive effect on the UK's trade with the new member states'? This is a highly misleading remark and it is to the great discredit both of the department, and of its secretary of state, that they should have kept repeating it.

The second later source to which BIS referred was the collection of submissions in response to the Foreign Office's invitation for views on the present balance of competences between the UK government and the EU.[19] This warrants a chapter to itself.

# 3

## What business told, and didn't tell, the Foreign Office

Of the 63 submissions in the trade and investment section of the Review of the Balance of Competences between the UK and the EU, 27 were from trade associations and professional bodies, nine came from individual businesses, and the remainder from devolved or foreign governments, from other government departments, from pressure groups and think tanks, from MEPs and other interested individuals, including just one skilled manual worker, who was also a sole trader.

They were, in the nature of the exercise, a self-selected group, so there is no way of knowing whether they might be biased in any particular direction. It may be significant that there is no formal written submission in this volume from the fishing industry which is thought to have been especially hard hit by the Common Fisheries Policy (CFP).[1] The only surviving cane sugar refiner in the UK, Tate and Lyle, made a submission which pointed out that the other five cane sugar refiners that existed in 1973 had disappeared, in its view because of EU protection for the continental sugar beet industry, so they could hardly be around to make a submission. The 'cultural industries', such as television, movies and online and audio-visual entertainments must surely have felt that they had been dealt a hammer blow by the French veto on the inclusion of any of them in the current Transatlantic Trade and Investment Partnership (TTIP) negotiations, but they were not represented at all. None of the submissions declared any interest by virtue of grants they or their members received from the EC, though a number might well have done so.[2] These grants are ultimately paid, of course, by British taxpayers, but they are received by favour of the EC, and branded as such. Intermittently, therefore one wonders whether as clients of the commission, they are wary of giving any grounds for criticism of it.

Whatever hidden biases there may be, all 63 responses were examined in the hope that some might include, or at least cite, evidence about how competences currently exercised by the EC had benefited UK exports, and hence provide some empirical support for the minister's claim. Very few of them did so, or even tried. Indeed, the striking thing about the submissions as a whole is the relative scarcity of systematic empirical evidence of any kind, on any issue, either given or cited, even though at one point the Foreign Office specifically asked for it.

## Business prefers the status quo

Despite the lack of evidence, the minds of most informants were made up on the two major issues. Trade agreements, in the view of a clear majority, are best negotiated by the EU and not by the UK government.[3] By contrast, they thought trade promotion should remain a national competence. Opinion on this latter point was unanimous. Since these views coincide with the present balance of competences, we may say that the majority of trade associations and businesses voted for the status quo.

A small minority were unconvinced of any benefits for themselves or the UK, either of the present balance of competences, or of the EU in general. The International Meat Traders Association, for example, said that it had found that 'countries like China and Russia prefer negotiations with individual states' rather than the EU, and complained of 'the lack of continuity' in EU staff. The British Art Market Federation described in detail how the EU artist's resale rights directive had reduced the EU share of world trade in art works, and had reduced most of all the share of the largest art market in the EU, that of the UK. The British Chemical Engineering Contractors Association considered the EU to be a rather unimportant market for its members. It reported that member firms work mainly in the UK, 'then it's the Middle East, North America, South America, Far East and Australia. There is little mainstream work in Europe and what there is is won by the local contractors in the main... The only area where we have had success is Norway.'[4]

While these and other submissions from the dissenting minority deserve attention in any final assessment, they are not relevant in the present context. We are searching for evidence to support for the minister's claim of substantial economic benefits of the Single Market programme, and they do not provide any. We will therefore focus on the submissions taking the majority view, since they are more likely to identify the benefits of the programme.

The Scotch Whisky Association was perhaps the most enthusiastic, and least critical of the EU's trade competence. The EU, it said:

> ... is vital to the industry's long-term sustainability, both as an internal market and as a strong voice in international trade negotiations... The EU internal market, in which one set of common rules applies, is immeasurably simpler than the alternative in which 28 different regulatory regimes would operate. EU rules, agreed with considerable input from UK officials and MEPs, impact on almost every facet of trade in Scotch whisky... The European Commission has been a strong and effective supporter of the industry's wider interests in international trade negotiations... the EU's use of the dispute settlement process and WTO disciplines more generally has been of considerable benefit to the sector... we see no issues which require subsidiarity or to be repatriated to national level.[5]

This submission is unique in that it alludes to the specific facets of trade regulation such as 'spirits definitions; protection of geographical indications... labelling; taxation; a standardised range of bottle sizes; holding and movement of excisable products; and environmental issues', where EU regulation has helped their members. It is also unique because other submissions, including many of those in favour of EU membership, and of the present balance of competences, mention only problems of EU regulation, while the Scotch Whisky Association reported none.

Presumably, they could, if pushed, have translated their enthusiasm into some comparative metric on exports of non-members to the EU, such as the Kentucky Distillers' Association or the Tennessee Distillers Guild, and perhaps shown how much more their own exports had grown as a result of the Single Market. This would have been of particular interest given recent reports of falling Scotch whisky sales in many important world markets, including a number not covered by EU trade agreements.[6] They did not, however, present any evidence of this kind. Simply to see if there is any to support the association's warm commendation, some UN Comtrade comparative data on whisky exports, from member and non-member countries, to the EU over the life of the Single Market is examined in Appendix C. It is less than reassuring.

A few submissions, like the self-nominated Senior European Experts Group and Business for New Europe pressure group, repeated the now standard data to show that the Single Market is very large, and very important for UK exports. Since every country in the world trades disproportionately with its near neighbours, information that the UK also trades a lot with its 27 nearest neighbours is not particularly illuminating when trying to discover how the Single Market might have improved UK exports, or what benefits its members might have obtained that were not available to non-members.

## Two exceptional evidence-backed submissions

Only two submissions came close to identifying specific measureable benefits that had flowed from EU free trade agreements (FTAs). Lloyds, the insurance broker, said that the EU's FTAs 'have benefited UK insurance', but declined to give the evidence that might support this claim. Instead, they singled out, as a commendable example, the agreement with Chile concluded by the EC in 2003. It looks like a rather casually selected example but it was a good one. It appears to have the highest increase in post-agreement growth of UK exports of all the EU-negotiated goods agreements (whose pre- and post-agreement export growth can be compared) since the UK surrendered responsibility for negotiating trade agreements in 1973. It is, one must add, one of a rather small number. Most EC agreements have been followed by a decline in the growth of UK exports to the partner country as may be seen in Appendix F.[7]

The services element in the agreement, and that is what Lloyd's presumably had in mind, came into force in 2005. Over the seven years since the agreement (2006-2012), UK services exports to Chile grew, in nominal terms, by 66 per cent while UK world services exports have grown by only 24 per cent. Over the seven years prior to the agreement, the difference was decidedly in the other direction. Services exports to Chile were virtually static, while UK world services exports grew by 75 per cent. UK services exports are just over half the value of goods exports to Chile, so here is a clear benefit, which may reasonably be attributed to the FTA. Unfortunately, the EU has not concluded enough FTAs with a services element in recent years to enable one to determine just how common this experience might be, and there is no data on UK services exports in earlier years to evaluate the impact of the few earlier EU agreements that included services.

The pro-EU pressure group Business for New Europe presented a number of what it called 'case studies'. Two of these cited empirical data which it thought demonstrated the merits of FTAs negotiated by the EU, and it then argued that the UK would obtain less favourable agreements if it chose to negotiate alone. The first of these referred to the FTA with Mexico. 'Since a free trade agreement was reached between the EU and Mexico in 2000', they said, 'total trade has increased by 187 per cent from €21.7bn to €40.1bn in 2011'. This increase might have been more accurately expressed as an increase of 87 per cent, but the main point is that this says nothing about the benefit to the UK, which is what the Foreign Office was asking for. If we look at the OECD dataset, we can see that while it confirms that from 2000 to 2011 UK exports to Mexico grew by 87 per cent in real terms, it also shows that over the 11 years from 1990 to 2000, before the agreement came into force, UK exports to Mexico grew by 209 per cent, also in real terms. Suddenly, the increase following the EU's FTA does not seem worth celebrating or even mentioning.[8]

Business for New Europe's second 'case study' referred to the EU's FTA with South Korea 'which came into force on the 1 July 2011 and… in the first 9 months… EU exports increased by €6.7bn or 35 per cent compared to the same period in 2007'. One assumes that the comparison with 'the same period in 2007' was for the very good reason that they might avoid the unusual crisis years 2008-2010. But it is still not clear why, when asked about the benefits for the UK, they should again refer to evidence from the EU as a whole. The figures of UK exports of goods to South Korea over these same years are readily available. In 2007 their total value was $6.9bn, while in 2011 it was only $5bn, a fall of some 27 per cent, in current value dollars. UK services exports to Korea are only available (as of September 2015) from 2005 to 2012, which hardly allows us to examine the impact of an agreement which came into force in mid-2011.[9]

The depressing aspect of the Business for New Europe 'case studies' is that one of the few attempts to identify a tangible benefit of the Single Market for the UK in these 63 submissions should rest on a rather misleading use of publicly available data. It is as if Business for New Europe are so confident of their case that they could not be bothered to check their own figures and, worse yet, confident also that no one else will bother to verify them either.[10]

## The trade agreements of small countries without heft or clout

Most business submissions supported the exclusive competence of the EC to negotiate trade agreements not with evidence, but simply on the grounds that the size of the EU provides 'greater bargaining strength' than the UK alone, or has more 'influence and weight', 'collective clout', and 'negotiating capital'. Moreover, non-member countries will, the majority claimed, inevitably favour negotiating to obtain freer trade access to 28 countries rather than to one, and this would, they thought, lead to quicker and more favourable agreements for its members including the UK. Hence without any evidence that these assumptions are correct, though with complete confidence, the majority concluded that it was best that the UK had surrendered its right to negotiate FTAs to the EC.

Any attempt to see whether these confident assumptions are correct must turn first to the WTO Regional Trade Agreement Information System (RTA-IS) database which lists all the trade agreements around the world since 1960 to date, with the dates they came into force as well as those still under negotiation. The ones that are of particular interest in the present context are those of small, independent countries that have little or no 'influence and weight', 'collective clout' or 'negotiating capital', to see whether they have been unable to negotiate as many FTAs as the EU. Four are worthy of particular attention: Chile, Korea, Singapore and Switzerland. Appendix E lists all their agreements alongside those of the EU, in chronological order, and distinguishes between those that cover only goods from those that cover both goods and services.

Table 2 selects some of the more notable agreements these countries have negotiated, and as may be seen, the absence of 'collective clout' does not appear to have prevented them concluding agreements, in rapid succession, with much larger economic powers, covering both goods and services long before the EU. Just for the record, one should recall that the EU does not currently have agreements in force with the US, Canada, Australia, China, Japan or India.[11] And to put the scale of the EU's negotiating efforts in perspective, one may add that the 2012 GDP of Japan, with which three of these small countries have concluded agreements, comfortably exceeds the combined 2012 GDP of every single foreign country with which the EC has concluded an FTA over the 45 years between 1970 and 2014.

This data gives no support to the view that small independent countries are less able to negotiate with large economic powers, or that the latter are less willing to negotiate with them, and no support either to the view that they will be slower in concluding such agreements. Those particular disadvantages for smaller, independent countries are clearly imaginary, and along with it surely the notion that the UK would be unable to negotiate agreements on its own.

None of the submissions supporting the majority view, including those of the CBI and TheCityUK, make any reference to any of these agreements, leading one to wonder whether they are even aware of them, for how is it possible for them to decide so confidently in favour of EC-negotiated FTAs without any evaluation of, or even reference to, the alternatives? Only one submission, that from Barry M. Jones, the self-employed skilled craftsman, makes explicit reference to any alternatives. He drew attention to the large number of FTAs negotiated by the European Free Trade Association (EFTA), which he claimed were superior to those of the EU, though he gives no evidence to support his view, other than his first-hand experience as a sole trader of the inconvenience and costs of EU rules.

One other submission generally supporting the majority view that deserves a mention was that of the Society of Motor Manufacturers and Traders (SMMT). It distinguished itself from the others by clearly recognising that the question of whether or not FTAs negotiated by the EC are better for the UK than those the UK might negotiate on its own ought to be decided by the same rigorous research standards that the SMMT, and its own members, apply in their own business decisions. It cut to the quick in the following passage:

> A key principle for SMMT is using sound economic analysis for determining which markets the EU should pursue trade agreements with. The role of UK government should be in advising and communicating its trade priorities to actors at a European level, based on a transparent method of economic assessment in determining key strategic trade partners. Within government's economic assessment of key trading partners, growth markets and sectors with comparative advantage, particular attention should be put on those markets where there is significant future potential to export.[12]

Presumably, although it did not say so, the SMMT's key principle also entails regular *post facto* assessment of past agreements to determine whether they are in fact having their intended impact, specifically on UK exports.[13] The key phrase in this passage is the qualifying 'within government's economic assessment of key trading partners'. The SMMT itself offers no assessment of any key trading partners, and therefore appears to be politely suggesting that it expects government rather than business to conduct the research that would enable one to judge whether the EC trade strategy was correct, and therefore to decide whether or not the balance of competences was beneficial.

The right hand column of Table 2 deserves particular attention. It shows that these four small independent countries have also been effective in including services in their agreements. According to successive UK prime ministers, the extension of export markets in services is a matter of special importance to the UK, and it is therefore useful to see whether this specific goal has been helped by the present balance of competences which most of the submissions from the business community commend.

**Table 2:** The major trade agreements of four small countries

| Partner country | Came into force (amended) | Goods & services |
|---|---|---|
| **Chile** | | |
| EU | 2003 (2005) | Y |
| U. S. | 2004 | Y |
| China | 2006 | Y |
| India | 2007 | N |
| Japan | 2007 | Y |
| Australia | 2009 | Y |
| **Korea** | | |
| India | 2010 | Y |
| EU | 2011 | Y |
| US | 2012 | Y |
| Turkey | 2012 | N |
| Australia | 2014 | Y |
| **Singapore** | | |
| Japan | 2002 | Y |
| EFTA | 2003 | Y |
| Australia | 2003 (2010) | Y |
| U. S. | 2004 | Y |
| China | 2005 (2009) | Y |
| India | 2005 (2010) | Y |
| **Switzerland** | | |
| Japan | 2009 | Y |
| Canada | 2009 | Y |
| China | 2014 | Y |

Source: WTO Database 'Participation in Regional Trade Agreements' rtais.wto.org

# The peculiarities of EU trade agreements

Figure 1 below compares the coverage of all the FTAs negotiated by these four small countries (in force as of January 2015) with those of the EU in terms of the aggregate GDP of the partner countries. The height of each column showing the size of the markets covered by the agreements is split into two halves with the left hand half giving the coverage of all FTAs and the right hand those agreements that refer specifically to services.

The EU FTAs are presented in two separate columns, the first on the far left being the exact equivalent of the others, in that it shows negotiations that the EU has conducted with other sovereign powers. This, however, seemed a less than fair comparison. The columns of the other four countries include their FTAs with the EU, while the EU's does not. Since the EU's efforts have been primarily directed towards creating freer trade amongst its own members, this may give a misleading impression. A second EU column was therefore added which includes the GDP of the EU itself as one of the markets covered by an EU FTA. As may be seen, it makes a substantial difference. The GDP of the EU itself is nearly three times larger than the aggregate GDP of all the countries with which it had successfully concluded FTAs which were in force in January 2015.

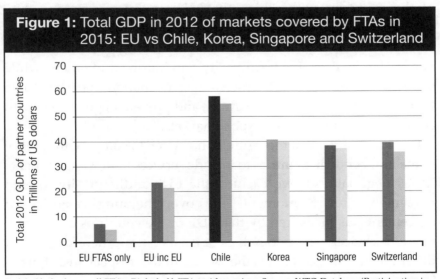

**Figure 1:** Total GDP in 2012 of markets covered by FTAs in 2015: EU vs Chile, Korea, Singapore and Switzerland

Left half of column: all FTAs, Right half: FTAs with services. Source: WTO Database 'Participation in Regional Trade Agreements' rtais.wto.org; World Bank, http://data.worldbank.org/indicator/

The WTO RTA-IS data files of the trade agreements, from which Figure 1 is drawn, are surprising on a number of counts. One of the reasons for the UK surrendering its right to negotiate FTAs to the EC is that, being so large itself, and having so much 'collective clout', the EC will be better able to negotiate with larger trading powers and blocs in the world than the UK. In the event, the EC seems to have given priority to negotiate with a large number of small countries like Andorra, Albania, Cameroon, Cote d'Ivoire, Costa Rica and the like, including the four countries with which it is here being compared. As a result, although it has a larger number of FTAs, the aggregate GDP of all its partner countries is, as the figure shows, far smaller than that of the other four countries. The contrast with Korea is quite striking. Korea has a very small number of agreements, but they are with countries with very large markets: India, China, Canada, the US, and of course, with the EU itself. The Korean notion of what matters in trade negotiations evidently differs from that of the EC.

These lists also throw a little doubt on the idea that the UK has been able to push the EU towards more open, free trade policies despite the protectionist inclinations of many other members. The CBI thinks the UK has been 'leading the drive towards a more outward-facing EU'.[14] The comparatively small size of the markets of the countries with which the EU has thus far managed to conclude agreements leave one wondering whether UK representatives may have been fobbed off with agreements with the Faroe Islands, Palestinian Authority, San Marino and others, while the member countries with protectionist inclinations have been able to drag their feet rather successfully, and prevent negotiations with countries with really large export markets.[15]

The main purpose of the figure is, however, to compare the ability of the independent countries to include services in those agreements it has negotiated. If we exclude the EU's authentically foreign agreements for a moment, the overwhelming majority of agreements, as measured by the GDP of the countries concerned, include services. The two halves of each column therefore do not differ greatly. Switzerland is the 'worst' in this respect, just short of 90 per cent of the value of the markets with which it has FTAs now in force include services. The EU, including the EU itself, is just over 90 per cent.

When, however, we turn to EU agreements negotiated with foreign countries, the first column, the proportion including services drops to 68 per cent, meaning nearly one third of EU FTAs with foreign countries do not include any reference to services at all. In terms of the absolute size of the markets opened, in some unknown manner and degree, to freer trade in services, the EU agreements total $4.8tn, whereas Swiss FTAs have opened markets of $35.8tn to their services exporters, which is more than seven times larger than those opened by EU negotiators. Singaporean FTAs have opened markets of $37.2tn, Korean of $40tn and Chilean of $55.4tn. By this simple, initial measure, the four smaller, independent countries seem to have been rather effective in negotiating FTAs, especially in services, while the 'collective clout' and 'negotiating leverage' of the EU has evidently counted for very little.

## Doubts about the credibility of business submissions

These figures raise questions about the credibility of the submissions of the business community commending the present balance of competences in trade negotiations. Did the CBI, TheCityUK and others ask themselves why the EU has managed to negotiate comparatively few services agreements? Did they assess the impact of those few? Did they assess the chances of the UK, negotiating by and for itself, securing significant services agreements with other English-speaking countries like Canada, the US, Singapore, Malaysia, India, Australia, New Zealand, and Hong Kong, most of which are entirely familiar with the common law, with British accounting practices, and with their educational and professional institutions? Did they have some method for deciding that potential partner countries would be more likely to reach agreements with EC negotiators, offering access to a large nominal single market which is, in reality, as we know, and they know, still fragmented into 28 distinct markets, by language and law, by national regulations (which remain of paramount importance for service providers), and by differing and unfamiliar educational and professional institutions? The idea that the EU's collective clout would persuade hesitant potential partners to forget all these barriers and hazards seems implausible. If it had ever been able to do so, there would, one imagines, be many more EU services agreements currently in force.

Figures about the number of FTAs do not, of course, say anything about their substantive content, so it may be that the EU's FTAs secure more substantial advantages for member countries than those of the four independent countries.[16] It may be, for instance, that the terms under which the UK services exporters can trade in the $4.8tn market that the EC has opened for them are very much better than the $35.8tn market that the Swiss have opened for their exporters and that the EU's 'influence and weight' have counted for something after all.

## On the scope of EU trade agreements

All negotiated FTAs are deposited with the WTO, and available online via the RTA-IS website, so it would be possible to form a judgement by comparing the coverage of both types. Indeed, it is only by doing so that one could give an authoritative answer to the FCO's main question about whether the present balance of competences between the EC and the UK government in trade negotiation is in the interest of the UK. As already noted, none of those giving confident answers to that question appear to have done so, but then neither has the UK government, nor the EC. No doubt, it would be a laborious task, but it is entirely feasible. In the meantime, we may simply note some of the characteristics of EU agreements from the sustainable impact assessments (SIAs) that have, since 1999, preceded them along with minutes of meetings and other related documents on the EC website. Independent countries do not publish any comparable evidence, but these SIAs give some indications about how the substance of EC agreements is likely to differ from those of independent countries.

The EC agreements are not only intended to increase trade. They are far wider in scope as their common prefixes indicate. They are not simply free or preferential trade agreements, but 'deep' and/or 'enhanced' or 'comprehensive' agreements. Some are described as economic partnership agreements. Originally, such agreements were the main, or even the only, instrument of EU foreign policy, and they retain this wider multi-purpose character to this day. Some were linked with the European Neighbourhood Policy whose aims were 'to encourage stability, security and prosperity in the neighbouring states without extending EU membership to them.' Others were part of the European Mediterranean Partnership, intended to create an 'area of peace, stability and shared prosperity between the EU and 10 Mediterranean partner countries.'[17] Many were therefore seen as a form of foreign aid, with no attempt to secure reciprocal tariff reductions, and included so-called flanking measures of technical assistance and aid from structural funds, enabling the EU to export its views of 'sustainable development and good governance' to various countries. Curiously enough, none of the UK business submissions supporting the present balance of competences mention these wider political aims at all.

Contemporary EU SIAs have three 'pillars' – economic, social and environmental – which they treat as equally important, though whether the negotiators treat them in that light is unknown. The social pillar commonly includes estimates of the impact increased trade might have on the economic and social rights of women, poverty and social exclusion in the partner country, and the environmental pillar includes estimates of the impact on the partner countries' natural resources and environment, and on climate change more generally. By contrast, the bilateral agreements of these independent countries are, as far as one can tell, much more narrowly and sharply focused on their own particular industries, and whether they can profit from a trade deal with that particular partner. Rightly or wrongly, they do not have any social or environmental pillars. It seems unlikely that when the Chileans concluded their agreement with the US in 2003, they checked out the implications for gender equality in the US, or when the Swiss concluded their agreement with China, they received assurances about its environmental impact.[18] It therefore seems fair to infer that they are both simpler and faster, and the speed with which their recent agreements have been concluded confirms the point.

By contrast, the EU agreements are necessarily cumbersome and slow. They are plurilateral before they can assume a bi-lateral form, since to bring its collective clout to bear the EC first has to co-ordinate, synchronise or compromise the interests of its nine, 12, 15, 27, 28 members with their vast variety of industries. This must itself be quite a feat when dealing with larger economies, even before its negotiators get to the table, and start throwing their collective weight around. It must be especially difficult for EC negotiators prior to the negotiation of a new service agreement. This will inevitably require some degree of mutual recognition of regulatory systems, of tax regimes, and since enforcement of contracts is an important part of services trade, of legal procedures, possibly of accounting practices and employment institutions, certainly of educational and professional qualifications of service providers. If we assume that the EC negotiators wish to present an intelligible and attractive offer to the potential partner's service exporters, rather than relying entirely on their collective weight, they would first have to make some sense of the immensely diverse regulatory/legal systems and business practices of 28 member countries, before they, or the potential partner, could know what is a quid pro quo, or what amounts to an attractive offer or an acceptable compromise.

Given the social and environmental pillars, the EC negotiations must inevitably also be more extended, but even when negotiating the economic pillar their interests are far more comprehensive and intrusive than those of independent countries since they may include the enforcement of competition policy of the partner country, their labour markets and labour conditions, and their protection of brands and other intellectual property rights. The example of Ukraine indicates that they may also of course have a geo-political dimension that the bilateral agreements of independent countries avoid. The Swiss agreement with Ukraine came quietly into force on 1 June 2012. The EU's agreement with Ukraine was negotiated at about the same time, but remained in a sort of limbo for a while for political reasons. The WTO still has not recognised it as 'in force', though in July 2014, the EC decided to anticipate the implementation of the agreement unilaterally, and it was later signed by President Petro Poroshenko.

On certain issues, independent countries have no basis for negotiation, no locus standi as the lawyers say. Currently, the main hindrances to trade are so-called technical barriers to trade (TBTs) and sanitary and phytosanitary measures or requirements (SPS). TBTs are regulations concerning certification of materials, testing and inspection of quality standards, labelling, ingredients, weight, size, shelf-life, packaging as well as the possible environmental impact of their use and disposal. SPS measures are those intended to protect humans, animals, and plants from the risks of diseases, pests, or contaminants, and they refer to the restricted use and tolerance limits of substances, their safety, labelling, hygienic and quarantine requirements, disposal and the like. The possible misuse of both kinds of regulation as a covert form of protection and a barrier to free trade has long concerned the United Nations Conference on Trade and Development (UNCTAD), WTO, IMF, the World Bank, the OECD, the ISO (International Organization for Standardization) and other international agencies, who have endeavoured to prevent their misuse by agreeing uniform, but voluntary, global standards.[19]

Since independent countries are usually only a small fraction of the trade of any negotiating partner country, it would be wholly unrealistic for them to engage in setting new standards and measures of either kind, and far more likely that, where the two sides differ, they will simply accept existing international standards from the ISO or some comparable body.[20] However, since the EU has 28 member countries, it can reasonably broach such issues in its trade negotiations, and if existing global standards are inapplicable or defective for some reason, it clearly has a better chance of persuading the other party to accept its own standards, and thereby make a positive contribution to setting new global standards.

Presumably the CBI had the social and environmental pillars in mind, as well as setting new technical and SPS standards, when it said that the EC operates on 'the principle of only signing off deep, comprehensive agreements with a very high level of ambition,' adding that this is 'a principle that the CBI fully supports'. This is, however, one occasion when one wishes the CBI had not decided to accept grants from the EC, since one might then be sure that they had conducted a thorough assessment of the costs and delays of the 'deep, comprehensive agreements with a very high level of ambition' that they prefer, and had compared the relative costs and benefits of doing so alongside those of independently negotiated agreements.

Whether their member firms, as well as other trade federations and their member firms, also think these wider and deeper issues should sensibly be included in trade negotiations must be in doubt, since there is nothing in any of their submissions to indicate that they have ever been asked to make such an informed choice. The inclusion of social and environmental pillars must help a few UK importers avoid unpleasant TV exposés of the lot of their suppliers' workers, but for most UK exporters the gains must be rather small. Quite apart from having to survive the preliminary intra-EU negotiations in which they are one among many, the EC itself, as a newcomer to the business of standard-setting, necessarily has to accept global standards laid down by the ISO and other public and private bodies.[21]

Once the negotiations are complete, the EC negotiators then have to answer to diverse NGOs, pressure groups frequently at odds with one another, to the Council of Ministers, and indirectly to the parliaments of 28 member countries since the Treaty of Lisbon, and to the European Parliament.[22] Since this ratification process has only been tested with relatively small countries like Ukraine, we have yet to see whether it will lead to delays with really large countries like the US and China. British business's submissions to the Foreign Office are, one must say, a remarkable and surprising, albeit tacit, testimony to their support for improving labour conditions in partner countries, to their willingness to subordinate their self-interests to the cause of limiting climate change and to the cause of European solidarity. Either that or they did not fully understand what they or the CBI were signing up to.

## Have EU trade agreements increased UK exports?

From all this it follows that it is not easy to compare the trade agreements of the EU with those of independent countries, and assess their respective merits. At the end of the day, however public-spirited EU negotiators and British exporters may be, the main criterion by which FTAs have to be judged is their results, that is to say, whether they actually increased trade as they were intended to do. The other goals can, after all, also be furthered by other means and other agencies. Only two of these submissions, those of Lloyd's and Business for New Europe, indicate any interest in what the impact of the EC agreements might have been on their or their members' exports, and give any chance of checking whether these agreements had actually helped them.

In an earlier study, an attempt was made to compare the rate of growth of UK exports of goods before and after EU FTAs negotiated on its behalf by the EC, with that of Swiss exports before and after FTAs Switzerland had negotiated by itself or with EFTA (Norway, Iceland and Liechtenstein). The results suggested that the Swiss agreements were far superior by this measure. In just five of the 15 countries from which we have adequate evidence before and after the EU agreement, the compound annual growth rate (CAGR) of UK exports increased. In the other 10 it declined. By contrast, the post-agreement CAGR of Swiss exports increased in nine of the 14 comparable Swiss agreements and fell in five. Moreover, the post-agreement increases in Swiss exports were, for the most part, strikingly larger than those of the UK. The most significant EC negotiating triumphs on behalf of British exporters over the 40-plus years up to 2012 - in terms of post-agreement export growth - have been Chile, Fiji and Turkey, followed by Lebanon and Papua New Guinea. There aren't any others.[23] Do these five agreements constitute such a remarkable track record for the EC's 40-plus years of negotiating effort? Are we seriously to believe that, on its own, the UK could have done no better?

In Appendix F this earlier comparison of Swiss and British post-agreement export growth has been replicated and extended to include Chile, Korea and Singapore with evidence from the UN Comtrade database. It shows, once again, that most Swiss agreements (11 out of 15) have been followed by higher growth of Swiss exports to the partner countries, whereas most EU agreements (10 out of 15) have been followed by a decline in the rate of growth of UK exports to the partner countries. In most cases post-agreement growth of Korean and Singaporean exports has, like those of the Swiss, increased while the post-agreement growth of Chilean exports to partner countries has, like British exports, more often than not declined. However, the post-agreement decline of Chile's exports is most probably explained by exceptional and unsustainable high pre-agreement rates of growth. The CAGR of its exports to China over nine pre-agreement years was nearly 33 per cent, to India over eight years was 42 per cent and to Australia over six years 28 per cent. There is no similar explanation for the post-agreement decline of UK export growth.

## On the services agreements of Switzerland and Singapore

For reasons already mentioned, it is not possible to conduct a similar study of the impact of EU FTAs on services exports. There are too few of them, and the historical evidence is insufficient. However, it may be useful to examine a few specific items of evidence that are available simply to see whether the arguments put by the majority of these submissions are convincing, or at least plausible.

The services exports of Switzerland may serve as an example. One imagines that, as a close competitor of the City of London, it would have been of particular interest to TheCityUK which represents the UK-based financial and related professional services industry 'at the corporate level'.

Swiss service exports to members of the EU over the years 1999 to 2010 grew, in real terms, at *nearly double* the rate of UK services exports to other members, despite the limitations of their bilateral agreements with the EU.[24] Swiss services exports to the world over these years grew in real terms by 114 per cent with a CAGR of 7.15 per cent while the UK's grew by only 70 per cent, with a CAGR of 4.95 per cent. These sharp contrasts, one would have thought, would have long since rung alarm bells during the meetings of TheCityUK's advisory council, and someone must surely have asked whether this might not be due in some measure to Switzerland's freedom to negotiate its own FTAs. It would hardly be unreasonable to suppose that there was a close causal connection. Why negotiate so many FTAs with a service element if there isn't?

Reasonable as it may sound, WTO data on world financial services exports, which is available the years 2005 to 2013, gives little *prima facie* support for this idea. The much larger UK exports of financial services grew by five per cent over these crisis-affected years, and the Swiss by only two per cent.[25] So their independently-negotiated FTAs do not appear to have given them any marked and visible advantage over the UK up to 2013, in financial services at least. The other services are presumably not of direct interest to TheCityUK, though it would have been courteous perhaps if they had given some thought to the larger UK interest.

TheCityUK's alarm bells should not, however, be switched off just yet. The performance of another competitor, Singapore, raises the same question, still more insistently. Singapore has a smaller GDP and population than Switzerland's, but with rather larger exports of financial services than the Swiss. It has been able, as we have seen, to negotiate its own FTAs with several larger economies such as Japan, India, the U.S and China, agreements which must remain a very distant dream for British services exporters. Over the years 2005-2013 Singapore's financial services exports grew by 19 per cent, far outstripping both the UK and Switzerland.[26]

Before arguing so confidently against independently-negotiated FTAs, TheCityUK may of course have conducted research which demonstrates that, despite appearances, Singapore's rapid growth of its financial services exports had nothing to do with the FTAs it had negotiated. Readers of its submission are, however, given no glimpse or citation of any such research.

## Are the British incapable of negotiating for themselves?

TheCityUK has, however, a final argument, occasionally mentioned in other submissions, which is that the UK is 'no longer equipped to conduct its own trade negotiations'.[27] Here then is a tangible benefit of EU membership, even a clinching argument for membership, since without EC negotiators, according to the TheCityUK, the UK would indeed be in a bad place, indeed locked into a bad place, and unable to negotiate any agreements at all, at least for a considerable time. If this were true, the merits or otherwise of the EC's FTAs rather fall to the wayside, since there is, in their view, no alternative to them at the present time. Since 1973, the EU has negotiated the agreements with a service element with six countries: Mexico (in force 2000), FYR Macedonia (2004), Chile (2005), Albania (2009), Montenegro (2010) and Serbia (2013). There have been no studies of the gains for UK service exporters from any of these agreements, but modest as they seem in terms of the possible world markets for the export of UK services, they are, one must admit, better than nothing. The UK service exporters might therefore be said to have benefited from EU membership since without it, according to TheCityUK, they would apparently have had no service-FTAs at all.

There is a grain of truth in TheCityUK argument. Judging by the quality of their own and other submissions, and by government publications over the years, there does not appear to be a large number of experienced trade agreement negotiators, analysts and commentators in the UK. But how could it be otherwise? Since the UK government surrendered its responsibilities for its trade negotiations to Brussels, and makes no attempt to monitor the FTAs negotiated on its behalf, there must be very little demand for their services. However, the idea that this is a reason for letting EC officials negotiate all UK trade relationships into the indefinite future, is stretching a point rather than making one, converting a short-term inconvenience into a formidable, insurmountable and permanent obstacle.

Elsewhere in its submission, TheCityUK proudly drew attention to the concentration of financial expertise and financial institutions in the City of London, and to the fact that it is by far the largest exporter of financial services in the EU. This makes it rather difficult to believe that the UK would be unable to find, in short order, sufficient experts with the relevant skills to conduct effective trade negotiations on its behalf, even among TheCityUK's own members, or those they employ.[28] The scarcity is not on the supply side but the predictable result of insufficient current demand. No one in the UK, including TheCityUK, currently seems to want to ask the demanding questions about such agreements or pay for the answers. Moreover, the argument ignores the fact that the preliminary analytical research for the EC negotiating teams is invariably outsourced to public and private consultancies, such as

Ecorys of Rotterdam, IBM, University of Manchester, LSE, the International Trade Institute of Singapore, and many more public and private agencies. There seems no good reason why the UK, if it had to negotiate by itself, could not do the same.

TheCityUK argument is also puzzling because in another, almost simultaneous, publication it was making the case for the 'vital' need for reform of the EC.[29] The 'core principle' of its reform proposals was subsidiarity, though not, needless to say, in trade negotiations. It was of course obliged to admit that:

> no case based on subsidiarity taken to the European Court of Justice for a ruling has ever been upheld. In practice, the principle of subsidiarity has too often fallen victim to a centralising instinct in the work of the Commission.

It then went on to propose a number of other structural reforms, some of which require EU treaty changes. Hence, we have to assume that TheCityUK is happy to entrust the City's interests in international trade negotiations to career officials of the EC even before any of the reforms that it considers vital have been realised, and even though, one might add, many in the City, including, one imagines, a few of TheCityUK's own members, have found various recent EU regulatory initiatives, such as the ban on short-selling, the financial transaction tax, the bonus cap on bank staff, less than helpful to their competitive position versus other financial centres around the world.

Such trust in the unreformed EC from hard heads in the City inevitably takes one a little by surprise. Perhaps TheCityUK has carried out background checks on, or held briefings with, the EC's TTIP lead negotiators, and knows that its trust is not misplaced.[30] Perhaps it knows that Ignacio Bercero, the head of the TTIP negotiating team, Marco Düerkop, a former German diplomat who heads the services negotiating team, and Martin Merlin, a former French treasury official, who heads the sub-group of regulatory co-operation in financial services, have acquired an expertise and understanding of the City of London's complex and varied financial institutions, and even perhaps a certain sympathy with them, during their careers in the commission that those actually working in the City would be unable to match. The careers of these lead negotiators are summarised in Appendix H. Since the language of the negotiations is English, they may well have studied in Britain, though the only mention of this experience is Señor Bercero's post-graduate degree from UCL.

Given that the Swiss, the Singaporeans, the Chileans and the Koreans have already completed many more negotiations about trade in services with major economic countries than the EC has ever attempted, it seems unlikely that the City and the UK lack the human resources and would be unable to negotiate as effectively as these smaller countries. TheCityUK seems to have frightened itself by imagining obstacles where none exist, and overlooking the considerable, indeed overwhelming, comparative advantages that the UK would enjoy if it were to negotiate its own FTAs in services.[31]

The failure of the CBI, TheCityUK and other UK trade federations to recognise the distinctive comparative advantages of their own country, and to notice what distinguishes it from other member countries, must be added to the other failures and omissions of their submissions to the balance of competences review. They declined to examine, analyse and reflect on the negotiating experience of independent countries. None of them assessed the post-agreement merits or demerits of EU FTAs for UK exporters. And none conducted, or at least presented or cited, any research to show that the EU's 'negotiating leverage' has produced faster or better agreements which have benefited British exporters.

At times, they resorted to what seems to be little more than gossip to support their arguments. For instance, the Federation of Small Businesses found it 'difficult to imagine the US would negotiate a trade agreement of the scale of TTIP with the UK on its own, as the UK can only offer a market of 60 million customers'.[32] The Engineering Employers Federation, making the same point, quoted an unnamed US official, who apparently said 'there would be "little appetite" to negotiate a bilateral deal with the UK if competence was at a national level'.[33] This unnamed US official first appeared in *The Guardian*, and has since appeared in many pro-EU publications, but has proved very difficult to track down. For the moment, we may only say that the notion that the US would be unwilling to negotiate 'at the national level', or with a country of only '60 million customers' is patently implausible. Currently, the US has 13 bilateral agreements in force, and the largest country of the 13, Australia, has in 2015 just 23 million customers.[34]

# The UK's lost years of freer trade

The submissions of the trade federations frequently leave one slightly suspicious, since they allow these federations to protect their own backs, and their own inactivity in the past, and quietly draw a veil over the many lost years of freer trade that their own members might have enjoyed if the UK had been able to negotiate for itself. Cover-ups do not come much bigger than this.

A rough estimate of the number of these lost years of freer trade may be made by assuming that the UK had managed to keep pace with the Swiss in negotiating independent agreements with other countries.[35] Since UK agricultural interests are less numerous, less powerful and less protectionist than the Swiss, it is not unreasonable to suppose that the UK could have done so, indeed it probably would have done so if it had remained a member of EFTA instead of joining the EU, since many of Switzerland's FTAs were in fact negotiated under EFTA auspices. Hence, the Swiss provide something like a natural experiment for what the UK might or could have done, except that the UK would, in all probability, have preceded Switzerland in its independent negotiations with Japan, the US and China. The UK has long been by far the most favoured European location for American and Japanese direct investors, and Chinese investors seem to be following in their footsteps. This is a clue about whom they find it easy to work with, and means there is a substantial constituency in these countries which is already used to working with UK service providers. English is, of course, the second language of both Japan and China.

In any event, had the UK simply kept pace with the Swiss, their exports to Turkey would have been assisted by an FTA four years earlier than they were, to Israel seven years earlier, and to Korea five years earlier. In many other cases, the number of lost years is of course still mounting, since Switzerland already has an FTA in force, while an EU agreement has still to be ratified and come into force, or is still being negotiated, or has not yet begun to be negotiated. Switzerland's FTA with Singapore came into force 10 years ago, those with Canada and Japan five years ago. Its agreement with China and Hong Kong came into force more than a year ago.

**Table 3:** The UK's lost years of freer trade, 1992–2015

An estimate based on Swiss and Singaporean bilateral FTAs with larger economies for which there is a later or no EU equivalent as of 1 March 2015

| Switzerland with | Date in force | Lost years* | EU equivalent |
|---|---|---|---|
| Turkey | 01-04-92 | 4 | 01-01-96 |
| Israel | 01-01-93 | 7 | 01-06-00 |
| Singapore | 01-01-03 | 12+ | nil |
| Korea | 01-09-06 | 5 | 01-07-11 |
| Canada | 01-07-09 | 6 | nil |
| Japan* | 01-09-09 | 5+ | nil |
| Hong Kong | 01-10-12 | 2+ | nil |
| China* | 01-07-14 | 1+ | nil |

| Singapore with | Date in force | Lost years* | EU equivalent |
|---|---|---|---|
| New Zealand | 01-01-01 | 14+ | nil |
| Japan | 30-11-02 | 12+ | nil |
| Australia | 28-07-03 | 11+ | nil |
| US | 01-01-04 | 11+ | nil |
| India | 01-08-05 | 9+ | nil |
| Korea | 02-03-06 | 5 | 01-07-11 |
| China | 01-01-09 | 6+ | nil |
| Chinese Taipei | 19-04-14 | 1+ | nil |

*to the nearest year

Source: WTO Database 'Participation in Regional Trade Agreements' rtais.wto.org

That, sadly, is still not the end of the story. These lost years of freer trade refer only to goods, so to them must be added the lost years of freer trade in services with the 15 countries with which the Swiss already have FTAs covering service industries in force, and the EU has been unable to reach any such agreement. The costs of these lost years of freer trade to UK service industries are probably already very large and still mounting, while the UK waits for the EU to amend its FTAs to include services. It may be a long wait.[36] Moreover, if the UK had been able to negotiate its own agreements, it is likely that they would have been tailored rather more closely to help the UK's own exporters than those of the EU as a whole. The UK would not only have had many more years of freer trade, but in all probability that trade would have been rather more advantageous for UK exporters.

All these lost years of freer trade are simply ignored by the confident majority of trade federations and the companies who submitted evidence to the Foreign Office, but any comprehensive evaluation of the relative merits of EC FTAs versus UK FTAs would surely have to take some account of them, as would any competent estimate of what UK exports would have been 'in the absence of the Single Market programme'. No such evaluation has been attempted, and with the solitary and notable exception of the SMMT, none of the trade associations and businesses who support the present balance of competences expressed any interest in conducting such a study. They apparently prefer to forget the many lost opportunities.

## Less than due diligence on the EU by British business

There are three things to be said about the submissions of the business community to the FCO balance of competences review.

The first is that since neither they, nor the UK government, nor the EC itself, have collected any evidence to demonstrate and measure the benefits of FTAs negotiated by the EC for UK exports, we may reasonably conclude that at present no one has the least idea whether they have been effective and helpful to them or not, and whether or not they have been more effective than those the UK might have negotiated on its own behalf. Hence none of them are able to give an informed, evidence-based answer to the Foreign Office's main question about the benefits for the UK of the present balance of competences in trade negotiation. After reviewing all their submissions, one must conclude that all of them are, or should have been, 'don't knows'.

The second is the near-unanimity of their submissions in favour of EU FTAs cannot be taken as a considered and informed verdict on this issue. It has instead to be seen as something else, as an affirmation of their faith, widely shared in the UK, in the benefits of freer trade, combined with the assumption, also widely-shared, that the Single Market is no more than a further logical extension of the freer trade of the Common Market years.[37] Given that the UK has surrendered its right to negotiate agreements, and as a good number of submissions point out the WTO seems permanently stalled, the EC is left as the only player currently able to do anything to promote freer trade. Not surprisingly therefore, it has their warm support.

The third is that there is a remarkable contrast between the rigour and standards successful businesses usually demand in their normal everyday decision-making, when investing in a new plant or product, or evaluating their marketing strategy, and the standards they apply when assessing a wider, public, national issue like EU membership or the Single Market. It is all too easy for outsiders to assume that they have given such national concerns as much careful thought as they have given to their own private interests, and they seem to want outsiders to believe that they have done so. These submissions demonstrate that this is far from the case. There is a striking contrast, even a complete disconnect, between the care and attention they pay to their decision-making in their own private affairs and their rather casual, ill-considered contributions to public decision-making. Since their opinions are likely to be taken seriously in any future debate on EU membership, and since they have far more funds at their disposal to advertise their ill-informed views than other participants, this contrast needs flagging.

In the present context, the most important conclusion to be drawn from this examination of business submissions to the FCO balance of competences review is that they provide no evidence to support the minister's claims of the 'significant economic benefits' to the UK of the Single Market. One can find strongly-held and widely-shared opinions, but not evidence, nor even leads to relevant evidence, other than Lloyd's reference to the EU's FTA with Chile. As one looks around for the missing evidence business declined to provide to support their views on the merits of EC-negotiated FTAs, one necessarily has to refer to the FTAs of independent countries like Switzerland, Singapore, Chile and Korea. As soon as one does that, the case for ceding responsibility for trade negotiations to the EC begins to unravel rapidly. Far from being a significant economic benefit, it seems more probable that the Single Market, and the dependence on FTAs negotiated by the EC it requires, has resulted in significant, and probably very large, economic losses to the UK which are continuing to mount.

At the end of this vain search for evidence to support the minister's claim, the one basic question that first started this investigation still remains to be answered. It is an interesting and important question: by how much has UK trade increased as a result of the Single Market programme, and how much less trade would there have been without it? The second part of this investigation attempts to answer it.

Since the minister left no clues whatever about the way he or his civil servants arrived at his doubling figure, we will have to devise our own approach to the question. Hopefully, it will give us some evidence-based estimate of just how near or far from the truth he might have been.

# Part Two

## The Paradox of Who Benefits from the Single Market

# 4

# What would have happened in the absence of the Single Market?

To begin to get some idea of what trade in the EU might have been 'in the absence of the Single Market programme', we will examine trade in the EU literally in its absence, that is to say over the two decades before it began, from 1973 to 1992. Since we now have 20 years of trade data since it was formally inaugurated in 1993, we may conveniently compare EU trade over the years 1973-1992 with the two decades of trading under its auspices, from 1993 to 2012.

Ed Davey claimed that EU countries trade twice as much with each other as they would do in the absence of the Single Market programme, which would mean, since trade embraces both imports and exports, that both their exports to and their imports from each other were twice as large as they would have been if the programme had never been thought of. However, we will, for simplicity's sake, examine only exports.[1] From a policy point of view, exports are much the most important half of trade. No EU programme is designed or required to increase UK imports, and the supposed benefits of the Single Market, like increases in GDP and employment, are primarily transmitted to the UK via exports.

Hence the first step will be to examine the growth in the value of the exports of EU countries to each other over the 20 years before the programme existed, and compare them with the actual growth in their value over the 20 years after the programme came into effect. If the minister's claim was somewhere near the truth, then we might reasonably detect a surge of some kind following the introduction of the programme, or at any rate a steadily increasing growth rate after it came into effect.

Of course, if absolutely nothing had happened in 1993, and no one had thought of the Single Market, exports would still have continued to grow, just as they had done over the previous 20 years. Thus, the problem is to assess just how much extra growth there may have been as a result of the programme. To do this, we will extend the exponential growth curve of actual export values over the years 1973-1992, to show what the growth of exports would have been over the years 1993-2012 if absolutely nothing at all had happened in 1993, and exports of these EU countries to each other had continued to grow exactly as they had done over the years 1973-1992.

This is, of course, a wholly improbable and imaginary reconstruction, though for analytical purposes, when placed alongside what really happened to exports from 1993 to 2012, it is an illuminating one. After making the assumption that the many variables that are known to affect exports such as variations in tariff and exchange rates, raw material, capital, labour and transport costs, production technologies, continued to vary exactly as they had done over the preceding decades, the exercise requires no further assumptions, and unlike models that are often used to predict future growth, requires no fallible human interventions, no estimates, no proxies and no less than reliable data files. Moreover, since we will be using publicly available OECD data, anyone who can use Excel can replicate each step of the following analyses, and verify or correct the conclusions with a few clicks of their mouse.[2]

A few caveats are necessary before beginning. First, while 1 January 1993 is conventionally taken to be the start date of the Single Market programme, some elements of it predate its official inauguration, and began to be phased in, over several years, after the Single European Act came into force in 1987, and it has of course been evolving or 'deepening' since 1993. However, the 20 years 1993-2012 are conventionally seen, and celebrated, as the years of its greatest impact and achievements, and hence it seems reasonable to distinguish those years if we hope to measure its impact.

Second, to make meaningful comparisons of EU trade over 40 years – 20 years before and after the Single Market began – we must of course hold constant the number of member countries. However, three of the founder members of the Single Market were not members of the EU in 1973. We are obliged, therefore, to insert an extra counter-factual, and backdate the entry of these three founder members of the Single Market, Greece, Portugal and Spain, as if their membership had commenced in 1973, instead of 1981 and 1986 respectively.

Third, the data used refer only to the export of goods since there is no data which would allow us to conduct a similar analysis of services. The minister referred simply to trade, but he too was presumably referring only to trade in goods, so this limitation is common ground. However, goods have been a declining sector of the UK, as of other EU and OECD economies, to varying degrees, over the decades examined. It is possible, therefore that an analysis of services might give different results, though not, one imagines, terribly different, given the EC report's observation that 'there is little difference between (the services) trade between EU25 Member States and trade between the EU and third countries'. In other words, the EC itself thought that the Single Market had thus far, (i.e. up to 2004 at least, the latest year for which the EC staff had data) had little effect on trade in services, and its benefits were largely confined to goods. However, as a postscript of this analysis, the limited and uneven available data on services exports will be examined in an attempt to discover whether they are likely to lead to different conclusions.

Finally, and almost needless to add, all these calculations assume *ceteris paribus*, as if the only significant change affecting exports of the founder members of the EU, of the UK, and of eight independent OECD members who are included in the later comparisons, over the past 40 years has been participation or non-participation in the Single Market programme.

## Intra-EU exports

Figure 2 shows, on the blue plot line, the growth in the value, in constant US(1973)$, of the exports of goods of 11 of the 12 founder member countries to each other from 1973 to 2012. The twelfth founder member, Luxembourg, has to be excluded for lack of adequate data. The continuous red line from 1973 to 1992 is the exponential trendline of exports of these countries to each other over these two decades. The serrated red line is the extrapolation of that trendline to 2012.

The $R^2$ measure of fit of this trendline of the recorded annual values of exports over the years 1973-1992 is 0.64, which is not very high, though perhaps not too surprising given the visible fluctuations in the value of exports over the period. It would certainly not provide a very safe basis for predicting exports over the Single Market years, but we are not trying to do that. We are trying to see what the value of their exports to each other would have been in an imaginary future in which absolutely nothing new happened over those years to propel or retard export growth continuing exactly as it had done over the previous two decades.

The serrated green line might be called the minister's counterfactual. It roughly traces what the value of EU members' exports to each other would have been if the minister's claim was correct; that is to say, if they had not been able to double because of the Single Market programme.

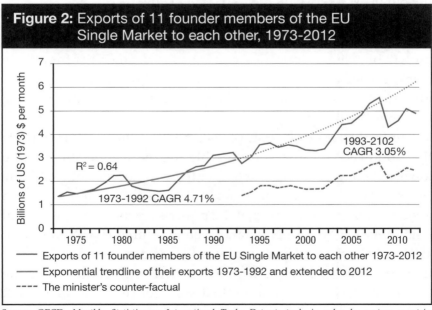

**Figure 2:** Exports of 11 founder members of the EU Single Market to each other, 1973-2012

Billions of US (1973) $ per month

$R^2 = 0.64$

1973-1992 CAGR 4.71%

1993-2102 CAGR 3.05%

—— Exports of 11 founder members of the EU Single Market to each other 1973-2012
—— Exponential trendline of their exports 1973-1992 and extended to 2012
---- The minister's counter-factual

Source: OECD, *Monthly Statistics on International Trade, Dataset: trade in value by partner countries* www.oecd.ilibrary.org/statistics (now discontinued in favour of quarterly, but this is based on monthly to 2012)

The first notable feature is that, over most of the Single Market years, real growth of exports has been lower than the growth projected from Common Market experience. The first significant decline below that projection occurred between 1999 and 2002, which happened to coincide with the launch of the euro, though whether this was a mere coincidence, or the new currency was in some way responsible, is irrelevant in the present context. This decline was followed by a rapid recovery between 2002 and 2008, but then there was an extremely sharp fall which coincides with, and no doubt was a direct result of, the financial crisis of 2008/9.

Since then, there has been a marked recovery, though by 2012 the value of exports was still some way below what might have been expected had export growth continued at the same rate as over the Common Market decades. Measured in 1973 US dollars, the total value of EU members' exports to each other over the Single Market decades was 91.25 per cent of what we might have expected had it been able to grow at the same rate as over the preceding two decades. In 1973 US dollars they were $1.36bn per month less than expected, and in 2012 US dollars $7bn per month less than expected. The real compound annual growth rate (CAGR) over the Common Market years was 4.71 per cent; over the Single Market years it was 3.05 per cent.

By both measures therefore, the 20 years of the Single Market do not seem to have been particularly successful in terms of the growth of member countries' exports to each other. Far from there being a detectable surge after the inauguration, or a faster rate of growth, they have failed to keep pace with growth over the Common Market years.

Plainly, the financial crisis of 2008 and the sharp fall in exports that followed are to a considerable degree responsible for the lower rate of growth recorded over the two decades of the Single Market. However, we can remove it from the comparison, and assume, rather debatably, that the pre-crisis boom was the normal Single Market growth path, and then measure growth only from 1993 to 2008, the peak year for intra-EU exports. When we do this, they are only 4.65 per cent short of their total value under the Common Market years, rather than 8.75 per cent, and the CAGR for these 16 years is 4.76 per cent, and marginally higher therefore than the CAGR of 4.71 per cent of members' exports to each other during the Common Market years.

Thus to decide whether the Single Market has contributed to the increase of exports of members to each other depends on where we choose to terminate our analysis of the Single Market years. If we stop before the crisis, exports have grown almost as much in total value as they did during the Common Market years, and the shortfall in their total value (versus what they would have been if the growth of the Common Market years had been reproduced) is almost halved from 8.75 per cent to 4.65 per cent, and the CAGR is 4.76 per cent rather than 3.05 per cent.

The green line on the graph that attempts to bring the minister's claim into the real world shows, as already noted, roughly where he claimed EU members' exports to each other would have been were it not for the Single Market. For this to be true, we would have to imagine that something else had happened in 1993 or thereabouts, to severely restrict and depress trade over the entire two decades of the Single Market, and keep it at or below its level over the Common Market decades. Clearly, that something else must have been much more severe and long-lasting than the financial crisis of 2008. But thanks to the simultaneous launch of the Single Market programme, according to the minister, EU exports did not continue along the green line and were able to grow as the blue line indicates they actually did.

Since the minister did not mention what this something else might have been, and no one else has noticed such an event, and since the UNCTAD data of the exports of the developed world as a whole gives no hint of such an occurrence, we may reasonably conclude that both it, and the supposed doubling of trade due to the Single Market, are figments of the minister's imagination. If he had wanted to give the House of Lords select committee an accurate account of trade under the Single Market, he would have said that, up to 2008, the CAGR of EU countries' exports to each other has been 0.05 per cent higher than that of the Common Market years, and this increase might perhaps, for want of any other explanation, be attributed to the Single

Market, though the growth of world trade was also higher over these years.

A brief comparison with the growth of world trade is helpful at this point, since if world trade had shown rather weak growth over the Single Market years compared with the preceding Common Market years, it might reasonably be said that the Single Market has been more successful than these figures suggest, in that it had helped EU members trade with each other quite well in more difficult world trading conditions. However, if we take UNCTAD evidence on world exports of all 'developed countries' (a category which includes most EU members) as a measure of trade conditions in the wider world, it shows they grew at a CAGR of 3.66 per cent over the Common Market years, and at the rather faster rate of 4.22 per cent over the Single Market years.[4] Hence it does not offer much support for this argument. Growth in the value of the exports within the Single Market also failed to keep pace with the overall rate of all developed countries' exports to the rest of the world.[5]

Limiting this comparison to the 16 pre-crisis years does not affect this conclusion. The CAGR of world exports of 'developed countries' as a whole over the years 1993-2008 was 5.64 per cent, while that of intra-Single Market exports was 4.76 per cent. The growth of world exports of developed countries is presented in exactly the same format as that of EU countries to each other in Figure 3.

The sharp contrast with EU exports to each other is immediately apparent in that the blue trendline plotting the real growth of the exports of 'developed countries' soars above that of the red trendline plotting their imaginary growth had they continued to grow at exactly the same rate as during the Common Market years, and remains above it even during the crisis and post-crisis years. There is no reason to be particularly surprised by this contrast, since world exports include of course exports to fast-growing economies in Asia. However, it does put the minister's claim about the Single Market in perspective: its members' exports to each other grew slowly compared with both their own past performance, as well as with their own and other developed societies' world exports.

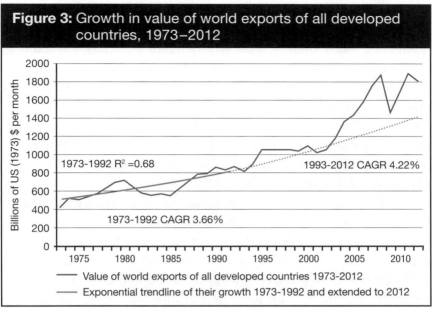

**Figure 3:** Growth in value of world exports of all developed countries, 1973–2012

Source: UNCTAD, International trade in goods and services/ Trade trends/ Values and shares of merchandise exports and imports, annual, 1948-2012: http://unctadstat.unctad.org

## Extra-EU exports

Our second step in trying to discover what might have happened in the absence of the Single Market is to examine the growth of the exports of EU members to other OECD countries that were not members of the programme. One of the main goals of the programme was to improve the competitiveness and efficiency of industries in member countries, and thereby improve their export performance in world markets. It is therefore worth examining their performance in these markets to see if they give any indication of improved competitiveness and efficiency.

There are eight for which adequate OECD data is available: Australia, Canada, Iceland, Japan, Norway, Switzerland, Turkey, and the United States. Four of these, Iceland, Norway, Switzerland and Turkey have negotiated substantial access to the Single Market, so while they are not members in the sense of sitting at the table and helping to make the rules, which is the sense in which the prime minister and others define membership, they are not in the same trading relationship as the other four non-members, since they have nil tariffs on goods, and presumably lower non-tariff barriers (NTBs). However, they raise the interesting methodological issue of whether they may contaminate the comparison by having negotiated more favourable access for their goods and services to members of the Single Market than the other non-members.

In the present context, this does not appear to be a telling objection since we are only examining them to see if the Single Market programme improved member countries' export performance in world markets so there seems no good reason why these four countries should not be included in the comparison. If the Single Market has improved these four countries' own export performance, it is beside the point, and if it has benefited EU exports to them it will exaggerate the benefits of the Single Market for its members - a point we must bear in mind but hardly grounds for excluding them from the small number of world markets for which data is available over the 40 years 1973-2012.

Figure 4 presents the exports of EU members to these eight countries over the same two periods and in the same manner as the intra-EU exports shown in Figure 2. The blue line shows, in 1973 US dollars, the actual growth in the value of exports per month over the 40 years 1973-2012. The continuous red line plots the exponential trendline of the value of exports over the Common Market years, and the serrated red line extrapolates from this data to show what export growth over the Single Market years would have been if it had continued exactly as it had done over those Common Market years. On this occasion, however, the $R^2$ is 0.48, a best fit that is even looser than that of the intra-EU exports.

Over both periods, exports of Single Market members to these countries were of higher value but grew much more slowly than those to fellow EU members. Their CAGR over the Common Market years was just 1.2 per cent, and over the 20 Single Market years still less, only 0.32 per cent. The EC report of 2007 discussed above pointed out that, whatever the intent of the micro-economic reforms of the Single Market programme, they had not improved member countries' export performance in world markets. These figures lend support to that conclusion.

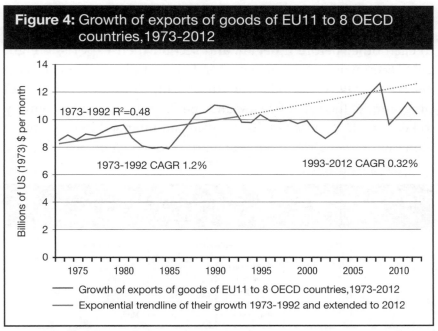

**Figure 4:** Growth of exports of goods of EU11 to 8 OECD countries,1973-2012

Source: OECD, *Monthly Statistics on International Trade, Dataset:* trade in value by partner countries www.oecd.ilibrary.org/statistics (now discontinued in favour of Quarterly, but I continued up to 2012 in Monthly)

In the present context, the first significant point is that the value of exports over the Single Market years again fell short of the value we might have expected had they managed to reproduce the growth of the Common Market years (apart from the pre-financial crisis surge peaking in 2008). In 2012 their total value, in 1973 US dollars, was 89.06 per cent or 10.84 per cent short of, what might have been expected had they simply reproduced their performance over the Common Market years.

Once again, however, we may terminate our comparison in 2008, and exclude the impact of the financial crisis. The CAGR over the pre-crisis years 1993-2008 is 1.66 per cent, and not only above the 0.32 per cent over the 20 years 1993-2012, but also slightly higher than the 1.2 per cent of the Common Market years. Likewise, if we only measure the growth in exports up to 2008, the shortfall declines to 9.45 per cent, meaning that actual exports were 90.55 per cent of what we might have expected had they exactly reproduced their Common Market performance.

We now have two pieces of evidence about EU members' exports in the absence of the Single Market programme: first their exports to each other before it began, and second their exports to eight OECD countries who were not members or full members of it. We also have two periods for measuring the Single Market programme, the full 20 years, and the 16 pre-crisis years. Simply to keep track of these results, they are summarised in the Table 4, along with the world exports of all developed countries.

**Table 4:** Summary of intra- and extra-EU export growth 1973-2012, with world exports of developed countries

| | 1973-1992 | 1993-2012 | | 1993-2008 | |
|---|---|---|---|---|---|
| | CAGR | % difference in value vs extrapolation of Common Market years | CAGR | % difference in value vs extrapolation of Common Market years | CAGR |
| Intra-EU exports | 4.71 | -8.75 | 3.05 | -4.65 | 4.76 |
| EU exports to 8 OECD non-members | 1.2 | -10.84 | 0.32 | -9.45 | 1.66 |
| World exports of all developed countries | 3.65 | +27.8 | 4.22 | +47.7 | 5.64 |

Source: OECD, *Monthly Statistics on International Trade, Dataset: trade in value by partner countries* www.oecd.ilibrary.org/statistics

The main reason for comparing intra-EU and extra-EU exports over the pre- and post-Single Market decades in this way was the hope that the differences between them would provide a rough, preliminary measure of the impact of the Single Market programme. If the programme had boosted members' exports to one another, it seemed reasonable to suppose not only that they would grow more rapidly after the inauguration of the Single Market, but that they would also grow more rapidly than their exports to independent countries who were not participants in the programme. No doubt, it would have been unrealistic to expect a sudden spike – the Single Market was phased in after all – but not unrealistic, if the predictions and rhetoric that accompanied it were to be believed, to expect a markedly higher rate of growth.

In the event, the differences on both counts are marginal. Post-Single Market growth of intra-EU exports is only fractionally (0.05 per cent) higher than pre-Single Market growth, with no sign of any surge, or any appreciable increased rate of growth, and the contrast with extra-EU growth is not illuminating.

One might perhaps draw a crumb of reassurance about the benefits of the Single Market from the decline in the growth of extra-EU exports over the 20 years of the programme (on the grounds that at least intra-EU exports did not decline as much) but over the 16 pre-crisis years of the programme these exports were growing reasonably, and the contrast with the shortfall in their total value versus the Common Market years does not suggest that intra-EU exports were benefiting significantly from the Single Market. One must also remember that the intra-EU exports of some member countries, including the UK, incur considerable extra costs arising from their membership of the Single Market. No allowance has been made in these calculations, or those that follow, for these additional costs.

The most striking contrast in the table is, however, between EU exports, both the intra and extra EU exports to other developed countries, on the one hand, and the significant growth of world exports of all developed countries. The minister's notion that members doubled their exports to each other is fantasy: cloud cuckoo land.

## UK exports to fellow members

The next stage of this exercise is to see how far the experience of all the founder members of the Single Market programme was shared by the UK. Figure 5 therefore reproduces the evidence of UK exports to the other founder members, minus Luxembourg, over the 40 years in the same manner as the preceding figures with the continuous red exponential trendline of exports over the Common Market years (which shows quite a high fit with their recorded values), and the serrated red line being the imaginary continuation of Common Market experience. The serrated green line is another glance at the minister's counter-factual, giving a rough idea of where he thought UK exports would have been were it not for the Single Market. It is a parting glance, I might add, since it can safely be excluded from serious discussion of the subject.

Like those of other Single Market founder members, UK exports also show a decline coinciding with the introduction of the euro, and with the financial crisis of 2008, but the striking, visible difference from Figure 2 above, showing all EU members' exports to each other, is the extent to which exports over the Single Market years have fallen short of the extrapolation from the Common Market years.

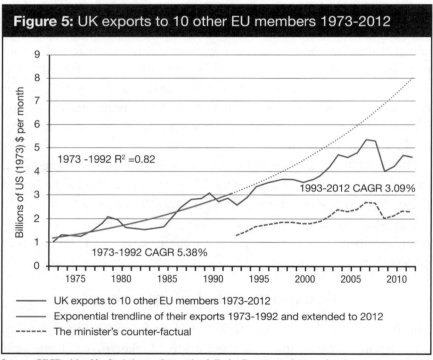

**Figure 5:** UK exports to 10 other EU members 1973-2012

Source: OECD, *Monthly Statistics on International Trade, Dataset:* trade in value by partner countries www.oecd.ilibrary.org/statistics (now discontinued in favour of quarterly, but this is based on monthly to 2012)

Whereas the total value of EU exports to other members was only 8.75 per cent less than those of the Common Market years, those of the UK alone to other members were 22.26 per cent less. While we have already seen that the Single Market cannot be counted a success in export terms for the EU as a whole, for the

UK it must be counted at the very least a massive disappointment, and not far short of a disaster. If UK exports to other members had continued to grow at the CAGR of 5.38 per cent as they had during the Common Market years, they would have been just short of US(1973)$8bn per month by 2012. In reality, they grew at a CAGR of 3.09 per cent over the Single Market years, and were US(1973)$4.6bn per month by 2012.[6]

The disappointment is due in part of course to the financial crisis. Once again therefore, we may calculate up to their peak pre-crisis year, which in the UK case was 2007, and again assume that the pre-crisis boom was all part of the normal growth path of the Single Market.[7] The CAGR over these 15 years was 5.3 per cent, and therefore only marginally (0.08 per cent) below that of the Common Market years. Over the first 15 years of the Single Market programme, UK exports to other members were performing reasonably well, meaning that they were almost keeping pace with the growth during the Common Market years.

And if we also count the shortfall in the total value of exports to other members up to 2007, it is only 14.6 per cent, compared with a shortfall of 22.3 per cent over the 20 years to 2012. However, whether calculated over 15 or 20 years the UK shortfall is still considerably larger than that of the exports of 11 founder members of the Single Market to each other. This confirms what has been demonstrated elsewhere, that impacts and benefits for the UK cannot simply be inferred, or scaled down, from impacts or benefits for the EU as a whole.

## UK exports to other OECD countries

Our next step is to compare UK export performance over the same 40 years under the auspices of the Single Market programme with its performance in other markets where it could not have enjoyed any of the benefits of the programme, other perhaps than EC support in trade disputes, since these other OECD countries were not Single Market members.

Figure 6 shows the growth in the value of UK exports to the same eight independent OECD countries that figured in the EU analysis above. UK exports to these eight countries were significantly lower

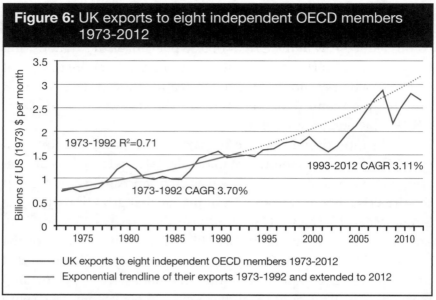

**Figure 6:** UK exports to eight independent OECD members 1973-2012

*(Chart y-axis: Billions of US (1973) $ per month, ranging 0 to 3.5; x-axis: years 1975 to 2010)*

1973-1992 $R^2$=0.71

1993-2012 CAGR 3.11%

1973-1992 CAGR 3.70%

—— UK exports to eight independent OECD members 1973-2012
—— Exponential trendline of their exports 1973-1992 and extended to 2012

Source: OECD, *Monthly Statistics on International Trade, Dataset: trade in value by partner countries* www.oecd.ilibrary.org/statistics (now discontinued in favour of Quarterly, but I continued up to 2012 in Monthly)

in total value than those to the 10 EU countries, and over the Common Market years grew at a slower rate, with a CAGR of 3.7 per cent versus the 5.38 per cent growth of UK exports to fellow members of the Common Market. This is a rather convincing margin, and might reasonably be taken to show the benefits of the Common Market for UK exports to other members.

Over the Single Market years it has been rather different. Even though UK exports to independent countries were also severely affected by the financial crisis, as the dip on the graph shows, their CAGR of 3.11 per cent over the two decades is only slightly less than the 3.7 per cent CAGR of the Common Market years, and fractionally more than the rate of growth of UK exports to fellow members of the Single Market which fell to 3.09 per cent over these same 20 years.

If we again calculate their growth only to their pre-crisis peaks, to eliminate the impact of the financial crisis, the fractional difference is the other way around. The CAGR of UK exports to independent OECD countries is 4.5 per cent while that to the EU over the years 1993-2007 is 4.91 per cent.[8] Over the 40 years from 1973 to 2012, UK exports of goods to fellow members of the EU and to independent countries therefore have contrasting, almost opposite, profiles. Exports to fellow EU members grew rapidly during the Common Market, and have been decelerating under the Single Market, while exports to independent OECD countries grew slowly under the Common Market, and have accelerated under the Single Market.

As a result of this acceleration, the value of UK exports to these countries over the two decades of the Single Market was 89.1 per cent of those we might have expected had they reproduced their performance under the Common Market, a shortfall of 10.9 per cent. This is less than a half, in other words, than the shortfall in UK exports to other EU members.

If we take the difference between the two shortfalls as a rough, initial indication of the benefits that might be attributed to the Single Market we must, in the UK case, subtract a shortfall of 22.26 per cent in exports to fellow members from a shortfall of 10.9 per cent to non-members which equals *minus*-11.36 per cent. This suggests that there has been no discernible benefit for UK exports to fellow members from the Single Market programme. Exports to independent countries have improved on their performance over the Common Market years markedly more than exports to fellow EU members. Unlike exports to fellow members they of course entail no costs for the UK taxpayer.

# Exports of independent OECD countries to the EU

The final stage of this analysis is to examine the exports of the same eight independent countries to the founder members of the Single Market. As non-members, these independent countries could not have enjoyed any of the advantages of the programme, or at least of those advantages which politicians of the main parties in the UK often bring to the attention of the British public, such as 'sitting at the table' and 'helping to make the rules'. However, four of them have agreements of various kinds with the EU, Norway and Iceland by virtue of the European Economic Area which makes them a part of the Single Market, apart from agriculture and fisheries, Switzerland by a series of bilateral agreements and

Turkey by means of a customs union. Hence it is not just possible, but highly probable that in exporting to the Single Market they have been helped by these agreements, so that they are not independent to the same extent as the other four.

Earlier, when discussing EU exports to these four countries, the idea that they might contaminate the comparison because of their links with the EU was noted, but they were not excluded from that comparison on the grounds that any contamination they might incur could only be in the 'right' direction, i.e. could only exaggerate EU exports. In the present context, however, of exports of these countries, the risk of contamination of the comparison is realistic, and several checks will therefore be carried out in a moment to see whether and how far the help these four countries have received from their agreements with the EU may have biased the results.

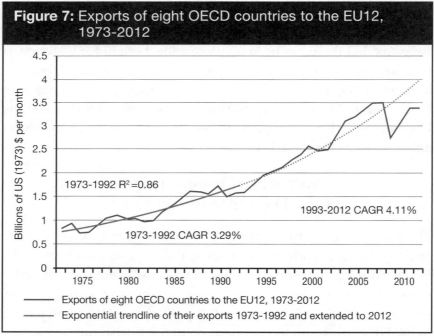

**Figure 7:** Exports of eight OECD countries to the EU12, 1973-2012

1973-1992 R²=0.86

1993-2012 CAGR 4.11%

1973-1992 CAGR 3.29%

Billions of US (1973) \$ per month

—— Exports of eight OECD countries to the EU12, 1973-2012
—— Exponential trendline of their exports 1973-1992 and extended to 2012

Source: OECD, *Monthly Statistics on International Trade, Dataset: trade in value by partner countries* www.oecd .ilibrary.org/statistics (now discontinued in favour of Quarterly, but I continued up to 2012 in Monthly)

Figure 7 shows, in the now familiar manner, the weighted mean of the exports of all eight independent OECD countries to the founder members of the Single Market. Oddly enough, a modest surge replaces the usual euro dip, though the fall following the financial crisis seems comparable to that in the exports of the EU and of the UK.

In the present context, the significant difference from the earlier graphs is that the growth in the value of the exports of these countries to the EU over the Single Market decades is visibly closer to the growth that might have been expected had they exactly duplicated their export performance over the Common Market years. Although in the final year of 2012, the value of their exports to the EU was 14.52 per cent short of the value if they had exactly reproduced their Common Market performance, the total value of their exports over the 20 years of the Single Market, the measure we have used throughout, was 97.95 per cent of the value expected from their Common Market performance, meaning they fell a mere 2.05 per cent short.

This is much the lowest shortfall we have encountered. We have already seen that the total value of EU members' exports to each other was 8.75 per cent short of the value expected if they had continued to grow exactly as they had during the Common Market years, while the total value of UK exports to other members fell short by 22.5 per cent. Supposedly disadvantaged non-members have, in other words, come closer to keeping pace with their export performance under the Common Market than the members of the Single Market exporting to each other, and very much closer than the UK, despite not having been sitting round the table and helping to make the rules.

If we consider only the pre-crisis years 1993-2008, the shortfall of 2.05 per cent disappears altogether and turns into a surplus of 2.93 per cent, meaning that – unlike the EU as a whole or the UK alone – the pre-crisis growth in the value of the exports of these eight independent countries under the Single Market exceeded their growth under the Common Market.

The CAGR of exports of these eight countries to the EU are also, as one might expect, distinctive. Over the Common Market years, it was 3.29 per cent but over the 20 Single Market years 4.11 per cent, and over the 16 pre-crisis years it was 5.47 per cent, the highest rate of growth of any of the export performances considered.

At the beginning of this exercise, it was suggested that if the minister was somewhere near the truth about the beneficial impact of the Single Market programme, we might reasonably expect to observe a surge in exports following the introduction of the programme, or perhaps a steadily increasing growth rate thereafter. The exports of EU members gave little sign of either. Their CAGR fell from 4.71 per cent in the Common Market decades to 3.05 per cent during the Single Market years. The UK registered an even greater decline from 5.38 per cent to 3.09 per cent, though both looked better when we measured only to the pre-crisis peak year of their exports to fellow members. In rather startling contrast, the eight OECD countries who did not participate in the programme fell only slightly short of their Common Market performance despite the financial crisis, and were doing rather better before it occurred. Non-members appear, in other words, to have benefited from the Single Market programme more than its own members.

Now we may ask how far this result may have been assisted by the inclusion of four countries, whose exports to the EU have presumably been helped by their agreements with the EU. One imagines that their inclusion has lifted the weighted mean of the eight countries somewhat above what it might have otherwise been. But by how much? Does their inclusion help to explain the startling paradox that the exports of eight countries that have not paid any membership fees, that have never sat round the table and helped to make the rules, have grown faster than those who have?

To consider this possibility, the growth of the exports from these four countries was measured separately from that of the four remaining countries that had no agreements in force with the EU – Australia, Canada, Japan and the US, both in exactly the same manner as the preceding comparisons. So that we are not overwhelmed with more charts, the results are presented in Table 5. The first line merely reproduces the result already described above, the second the four countries which had no agreements in force with the EU over the period, and the third line shows the weighted mean of the four countries whose exports to the EU may have been helped by their agreements with the EU. The results up to the eve of the financial crisis are shaded.

**Table 5:** Growth of Exports of three groups of countries to the EU Single Market 1973-2012 compared in 1973US$

| | CAGR 1973-1992 | CAGR 1993-2012 | Shortfall in 2012 | CAGR 1993-2008 | Shortfall in 2008 |
|---|---|---|---|---|---|
| 8 EU non-members Austrailia, Canada, Iceland, Japan, Norway, Turkey, Switzerland, US | 3.3 | 4.1 | 2.1 | 5.5 | +3.0 |
| 4 independents without EU agreements Austrailia, Canada, Japan, US | 3.4 | 4.1 | 4.7 | 5.6 | +1.0 |
| 4 countries with EU agreements Iceland, Norway, Turkey, Switzerland | 3.1 | 4.0 | 6.2 | 4.6 | -9.1 |

Source: OECD, *Monthly Statistics on International Trade, Dataset: trade in value by partner countries* www.oecd.ilibrary.org/statistics

The results suggest that the inclusion of the countries with trade agreements with the EU among the independent countries did not lift their weighted mean and give a misleading result. The results of the four independent countries without EU agreements in line two differ from the eight only in that the pre-crisis shortfall, or more precisely surplus, is rather smaller and the shortfall in 2012 is rather larger. The CAGRs are almost identical.

The surprise of these results is that the exports of the four countries which one expected to have been helped by their agreements with the EU did not grow as rapidly as those which had no agreements with the EU at all.[9] Their pre-crisis and two-decade CAGRs were both lower than those of the eight countries, and their shortfalls on their Common Market performance were both larger. If anything therefore, they lowered the mean rate of growth when they were included among the eight independent countries. Hence, they do not help to explain why non-members appear to have benefited more from the Single Market than its own members. They leave the paradox unresolved.

# A collective portrait of the Single Market's failure and its paradox

We have covered a fair amount of ground and used two measures of growth of five sets of exports over the two decades before and after the Single Market. The first is the shortfall in the total value of exports if they had exactly reproduced their growth over the Common Market years; the second is the CAGR over the two decades before and after the inauguration of the Single Market. It therefore may be helpful to present the results side by side to make comparison easier. The result is given in Figure 8.

The dark blue columns show the percentage growth in the total value of exports over the 20 years of the Single Market. The light blue columns show the growth up to the peak year before the financial crisis (this being 2008 in all cases except to the UK when it is 2007). The figures in the columns give the CAGR over the same periods, and the yellow figures at the base of the dark blue column give the CAGR over the Common Market decades.

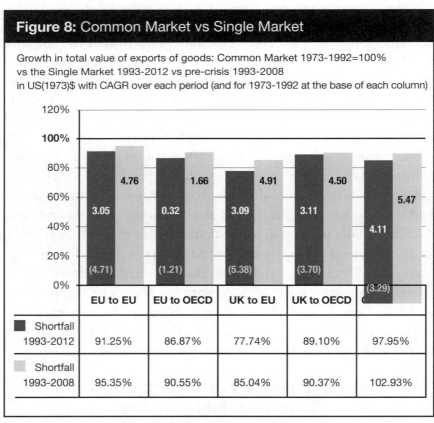

**Figure 8:** Common Market vs Single Market

Growth in total value of exports of goods: Common Market 1973-1992=100% vs the Single Market 1993-2012 vs pre-crisis 1993-2008
in US(1973)$ with CAGR over each period (and for 1973-1992 at the base of each column)

| | EU to EU | EU to OECD | UK to EU | UK to OECD | |
|---|---|---|---|---|---|
| Shortfall 1993-2012 | 91.25% | 86.87% | 77.74% | 89.10% | 97.95% |
| Shortfall 1993-2008 | 95.35% | 90.55% | 85.04% | 90.37% | 102.93% |

Source: OECD, *Monthly Statistics on International Trade, Dataset: trade in value by partner countries* www.oecd.ilibrary.org/statistics (now discontinued in favour of Quarterly, but I continued up to 2012 in Monthly)

If exports of every group over the Single Market decades had grown by exactly the same amount as they had done over the Common Market years, the dark blue columns would all be at the accentuated line of 100 per cent. None of them are, showing that exports of every group have grown less than we might have expected had they grown as much as they did over the 20 Common Market years, and by how much. However, if we eliminate the impact of the financial crisis of 2008, by measuring export growth only to that year (or in the UK case to 2007), all groups considered perform rather better (as shown by the light blue columns) but only the exports of the eight independent OECD countries grow more than they did over the Common Market years, and hence exceed 100 per cent. Likewise, as one might expect, the CAGR in the value of exports after eliminating the impact of the financial crisis is higher in every case than the CAGR over the 20 years of the Single Market from 1993-2012.

The peculiarities of the UK emerge more clearly in this composite comparative profile. Whilst it had the highest rate of export growth under the 20 years of the Common Market, as indicated by the bracketed (5.38) at the base of the dark blue column, it has fallen further short of its performance over those years than any other group, whether measured either to 2012 in the dark blue column, or to 2008 in light blue. Its exports to the EU are therefore also unique in having a CAGR in the pre-crisis years – in the years when the Single Market was working as it was supposed to work and undisturbed by a financial crisis – that is less than that of the Common Market years. Its exports to the EU also appear to have suffered more from the financial crisis than any other, as indicated both by differences between the dark and light blue columns of the total value of exports over the 20 years and the pre-crisis years, and by the CAGRs over the two periods.

In sum, for the UK the Single Market has been a vastly disappointing era in terms of the growth of the exports of its goods to other members. It compares unfavourably not only with the growth of its exports during the Common Market decades and with the growth of UK exports to non-member countries, but also with growth of exports to the Single Market of many OECD countries that are not members of the EU.

This final conclusion is counter-intuitive, and profoundly paradoxical. It flies in the face of the claims about the advantages of the Single Market for UK trade that have been made over many years by Britain's political leaders. Perhaps it ought not to have come as much of a surprise, since it has been emerging slowly but surely over two decades in the trade data regularly published by the OECD, and this data is standard fare for *The Economist* and the *Financial Times* and the financial pages of the other quality newspapers. Somehow or other however, it never seems to have provoked any interest or comment, or any attempt to reassess the much-advertised merits of the Single Market. For some reason, it seems to be above and beyond such mundane empirical verification.

Few British publications have recognised just how far the Single Market has fallen short of the optimistic predictions of the GDP gains that Paolo Cecchini derived from his model in 1988 – up to 6.5 or 7 per cent over five or six years. The EC estimated that by 2002, the overall positive impact of the Single Market had been of the order of 1.5 to 2 per cent of GDP. Eichengreen and Boltho examined this estimate and decided that 'as an upper estimate... perhaps half of the gains, as estimated by the commission in 2002, might not have been obtained in its absence' of the Single Market; which is to say their upper estimate of the gains from the Single Market is between 0.75 and one per cent of EU GDP.[10]

In 2011, in the seventh edition of a textbook on the European Union for school and university use, Ali El-Agraa, a professor at Fukuoka University, and his co-author Brian Ardy concluded that the impact of the Single Market was 'significant, but far from earth-shattering... The idea that [it] would transform EU economic performance has proved to be wide of the mark: there is no indication in the growth of output or productivity over this period that would support this contention'.[11] They did not make any comparisons with the non-members of the Single Market, so the paradox of their rather better export performance passed them by.

Why it has escaped notice and comment for so long is a bit of a mystery. It certainly did not require any sophisticated calculations. A minor reordering of the monthly data routinely published by the

OECD would have been sufficient, as presented in Table 6 below. This shows, in 1993 US dollars, the growth of the exports of a number of larger trading nations to the 12 founder members of the Single Market, alongside founder members' exports to each other. Non-members and members are, it is true, not exactly matched with one another, since individual EU member countries cannot of course export to themselves. While the exports of outsiders are therefore to all 12 founder members, the EU members' exports are to the other 11, though since we are looking at the relative growth in the same market, this mismatch is unlikely to be wildly misleading.

**Table 6:** Growth of Exports of three groups of countries to the EU Single Market 1973-2012 compared in 1973US$

|  | % real growth | CAGR% | Total value in 2012 $USbn |
|---|---|---|---|
| China | 664 | 11.30 | 163.3 |
| Russia | 387 | 8.69 | 105.7 |
| Brazil | 343 | 8.15 | 44.7 |
| India | 276 | 7.22 | 44.3 |
| Turkey | 250 | 6.81 | 77.0 |
| Korea | 199 | 5.94 | 43.0 |
| Australia | 190 | 5.76 | 37.9 |
| Mexico | 185 | 5.66 | 31.5 |
| S. Africa | 165 | 5.27 | 26.8 |
| Singapore | 145 | 4.84 | 35.2 |
| Canada | 115 | 4.11 | 34.6 |
| US | 114 | 4.09 | 342.0 |
| Switzerland | 102 | 3.77 | 148.5 |
| Norway | 92 | 3.49 | 36.8 |
| Hong Kong | 81 | 3.16 | 38.6 |
| **UK** | **72** | **2.90** | **175.0** |
| **EU mean** | **66** | **2.71** | **183.0** |
| Japan | 47 | 2.04 | 63.2 |
| Iceland | 44 | 1.93 | 1.5 |
| Israel | 37 | 1.68 | 30.2 |
| Taiwan | 30 | 1.40 | 18.6 |

Source: www.oecdilibrary.org.OECDdatabase Monthly Statistics of International Trade doi:10.1787/data-02279

The figures in this table are, one might note, consistent with the earlier calculations of what would have happened in the absence of the Single Market. Six of the eight independent OECD countries in the earlier calculations have had higher rates of growth than the EU mean and the UK, and only two have lower rates. Three of the 20 countries, Switzerland, Norway and Iceland, have Single Market access, Turkey has a customs union and two more, Mexico and South Africa, have trade agreements with the EU, both since 2000. (Korea also has an FTA with the EU, but it came into force in mid-2011, and can hardly have affected its exports up to 2012.) As a group these five countries are not particularly distinguished, as one might expect if this access and these agreements had yielded significant trade advantages over non-members.

Three of the countries listed – Turkey, Norway and Switzerland – have become stock examples in the 'Brexit isn't worth it' literature warning the British of their plight if they were to leave the EU.[12] For some reason, the authors of these warnings invariably forget to mention that the exports of all three of them have grown at a faster rate than those of the UK over the first two decades of the Single Market. And of course, after warning of the perils of Brexit, they also forget to mention the growth of the exports of the other 12 non-members.

Overall, as they stand, these figures offer little support to the argument that membership of the Single Market is essential if the UK is to maintain or increase the rate of growth of its exports to the Single Market. Since this is the principal argument for continued UK membership of the EU, these figures deserve careful examination, so that the reasons why the Single Market seems to have been of more benefit to non-members than to its own members might be understood and explained, and the paradox thereby resolved.

# 5

# Is there a single market in services?

All of the evidence and comment in the preceding chapter refers to the export of goods, and therefore gives only a partial view of the impact of the Single Market, since trade in services is a much larger sector of the UK economy, though it currently provides a lower proportion, 38.5 per cent, of all UK exports. These cannot, however, be examined in a similar manner since the OECD only began recording services exports to most partner countries in 1999. A few countries published figures for earlier years, but even for later years, cross-national comparative investigations are stymied by the unevenness and irregularity of the data.[1] Studies of 'what might have been' of the kind conducted above from 1973 are therefore out of the question.

This is a serious blow to any attempt to identify the benefits of the Single Market, especially in the case of the UK since its balance of payments in services is, unlike that in goods, in surplus both to the EU and to the rest of the world. It is therefore not unreasonable to suppose that the Single Market might have had benefits for UK service industries that have not been enjoyed by its manufacturing industries. Successive British prime ministers have been convinced that this is so, and it is for that reason, one assumes, that they have continuously pressed for the extension of the Single Market in services. However, without adequate historical evidence, it will be difficult to identify the benefits of the Single Market for services exports.

The EC report of 2007 was not particularly encouraging about these benefits. As noted earlier, one of its more startling findings was its comparison of services traded intra and extra-EU in 2004, which showed that 'there is little difference between trade (in services) between EU25 member states and trade between the EU and third countries.' They supported this finding with a histogram which showed that, in 2004, intra-EU exports were about six or seven per cent of EU GDP, while extra-EU exports were roughly nine per cent, which suggested to them, as they politely put it, 'that the internal market does not yet fully play its role in the services sectors'.[2]

Somewhat surprisingly, the EU statistical office Eurostat does not provide a continuous, accessible data series of the ratio of intra- and extra-EU exports as a percentage of GDP to monitor the integration of the Single Market in services. However, in the January 2015 update of their online Statistical Yearbook they again refer to it, noting that intra-EU trade in goods as a proportion of GDP is 'two thirds higher than exports to non-member countries', from which they infer that the Single Market in goods is highly integrated.[3] In the later section on services they observe that, by contrast, intra-EU trade is only 55.2 per cent of exports, and imply that there had been little change over the intervening eight years.[4]

OECD data, however, allow us to put together a substitute for the missing Eurostat time series, albeit with a few absent entries, consisting of the intra-EU and extra-EU exports of the 12 founder members of the Single Market as a proportion of their GDP over the years from 2002 to 2012. They are shown in Table 7. Intra-EU exports are to the other 11 founder members plus the eight other members for whom there is a fairly continuous set of figures over these years. Three of the eight joined in 1995 (Austria, Finland and Sweden), and five in 2004 (Czech Republic, Hungary, Poland, Slovakia and Slovenia). A few entries were missing, most of them marked 'non-publishable and confidential value' but these were, as the OECD confirmed to me in writing, nonetheless included in the world tables used to calculate the extra-EU exports. These missing entries were filled by giving the import figures, i.e. imports from Germany on the Swedish file replaced the missing German exports to Sweden. Substitutions of this kind were necessary in more than a third of all cells, 892 out of 2,508. They are far from ideal since the figures are collected by different

**Table 7:** Intra- and extra-EU services exports of 12 founder members of the Single Market as a proportion of EU GDP 2002-2012 in current value US$bn

| | Intra-EU: exports to 19 other members | As % of EU GDP | Extra-EU: exports to rest of world | As % of EU GDP | GDP in current PPPs US$bn | Per cent difference |
|---|---|---|---|---|---|---|
| 2002 | 351.6 | 3.58 | 287.5 | 2.93 | 9807.2 | 0.65 |
| 2003 | 431.7 | 4.30 | 344.8 | 3.43 | 10050.4 | 0.86 |
| 2004 | 525.1 | 4.99 | 413.5 | 3.93 | 10523.8 | 1.06 |
| 2005 | 562.0 | 5.08 | 457.6 | 4.14 | 11058.7 | 0.94 |
| 2006 | 635.1 | 5.30 | 506.1 | 4.22 | 11990.3 | 1.08 |
| 2007 | 756.6 | 5.98 | 615.2 | 4.87 | 12643.5 | 1.12 |
| 2008 | 821.5 | 6.25 | 677.5 | 5.16 | 13142.1 | 1.10 |
| 2009 | 744.8 | 5.79 | 630.4 | 4.90 | 12869.1 | 0.89 |
| 2010 | 766.3 | 5.83 | 662.5 | 5.04 | 13144.5 | 0.79 |
| 2011 | 855.0 | 6.25 | 755.7 | 5.53 | 13672.6 | 0.73 |
| 2012 | 817.0 | 5.87 | 753.3 | 5.41 | 13932.5 | 0.46 |

Note: Missing export entries were filled by imports from that country in the cases of German exports to Sweden, Finland & Slovenia 2002-12; Spanish exports to Austria, Belgium, Greece, Ireland, Luxembourg, Portugal , Finland, Slovakia, and Slovenia 2002-2005 plus Slovakia 2007 and Slovenia 2006-2012; Greek exports to Slovakia 2003-5, 2007, Slovenia, 2003, 2006; and for Irish exports to Italy in 2009, to Greece, 2002, 2006-7, to Portugal 2002, 2005.
NB five of the '19 other members' only fully joined the EU in 2004.

Sources: The export, and import, figures are taken from the datafiles of the individual member countries. OECD (2014), "Trade in services - EBOPS 2002", OECD Statistics on International Trade in Services (database). DOI: 10.1787/data-00274-en The GDP figures are taken from National Accounts at a Glance 2014 Gross domestic product, current PPPs, Last updated: 30-Jan-2014© OECD 2014. www.oecd-ilibrary.org

agencies, no doubt using different methodologies. And exports are usually measured FOB and imports CIF (FOB means 'free on board', separated from insurance and freight; 'CIF' means 'cost, insurance and freight') and so it is a different measurement. However, they are probably better than any reconstructed estimate.

The EC's chosen index of the degree of integration of the Single Market in services is the difference between the first two shaded columns, which is given in the third. As may be seen, the difference is small. Intra-EU exports have been slightly larger over these 11 years, climbing to around one per cent of EU GDP over the years 2004-8 and thereafter trailing away, so that the Single Market in services was, by this index, marginally less integrated in 2012 than it was in 2002.

Parity between the two figures would mean that a Single Market in services effectively does not exist, and so it looks as if having emerged gingerly in the first decade of the century, it then began to disappear, and in 2012, the last year for which data is available, seemed on the brink of disappearing altogether. The repeated efforts of successive British prime ministers to 'extend' it do not seem to have had much effect. The financial crisis might perhaps be responsible in some way, and to some degree, though the two columns giving the actual value of exports in billions of dollars show only slight dips in 2009 and 2010 by contrast with steep falls in goods exports noted earlier.

Some further insight into the nature of the Single Market, and the benefits of it for the UK and other members, can be obtained from the breakdown of the intra- and extra-EU services exports of the 12 founder member countries to each other and to eight other EU members, compared with their exports to the rest of the world, shown in Table 8.

The first striking feature of this table is the large variation in growth rates of the intra-EU exports of member countries, which suggests that the Single Market has had a far from uniform impact on all its members. Cecchini, and the model-builders who have subsequently provided optimistic predictions for the EC, almost invariably refer to gains for the EU as whole. In doing so, they are all misleading. Since there are similar, though by no means identical, variations in extra-EU exports, it seems more likely that the dynamics of these variations have little or nothing to do with the Single Market.

While the UK has been the largest exporter of services of the 12 founder members, its intra-EU exports have been of lower value than those of Germany and France, and as a proportion of total exports, its intra-EU exports have been lower than those of any other member. In this sense, the UK is the least integrated member of the Single Market in services. UK exports have also grown very slowly over these 11 years by comparison with those of most other

**Table 8:** Growth of intra- and extra-EU services exports of 12 founder members of Single Market, 2002-2012

Intra is to each other and to 8 other current EU members*
Extra is to the rest of the world
Compound Annual Growth Rate in US (2002) $, and value in 2012 in US(2012) $bn

| Intra-EU exports | | | Extra-EU exports | | |
|---|---|---|---|---|---|
| | CAGR % | Value in 2012 $bn | | CAGR % | Value in 2012 $bn |
| Ireland | 12.14 | 65.2 | Ireland | 12.58 | 50.8 |
| Luxembourg | 10.23 | 49.5 | Luxembourg | 11.78 | 22.8 |
| France | 8.50 | 114.9 | Portugal | 9.70 | 7.9 |
| Germany | 7.19 | 132.2 | Belgium | 9.70 | 37.8 |
| Belgium | 6.76 | 63.8 | Netherlands | 8.90 | 58.2 |
| Spain | 5.98 | 92.2 | Denmark | 8.88 | 38.6 |
| Portugal | 5.24 | 16.6 | Germany | 7.95 | 138.2 |
| Netherlands | 4.93 | 75.3 | UK | 6.48 | 181.2 |
| Denmark | 4.71 | 27.6 | Italy | 6.41 | 52.6 |
| UK | 4.32 | 110.7 | Spain | 6.30 | 45.5 |
| Greece | 2.30 | 16.7 | France | 5.64 | 101.3 |
| Italy | 0.89 | 52.5 | Greece | 4.45 | 18.7 |

*Austria, Finland and Sweden who joined in 1995, and Czech Republic, Hungary, Poland, Slovakia and Slovenia who joined in 2004.

Source: OECD Dataset: Trade in services, www.oecd.ilibrary.org/statistics

members, especially its intra-EU exports. As may be seen, only those of Greece and Italy grew more slowly. Its extra-EU exports grew at a slightly faster pace. However, the more important point is that this contrast between the slow growth of intra-EU exports and the faster growth of extra-EU is shared to different degrees by 10 other members. Only France has seen faster growth of its intra-EU services exports.

The importance of this disparity can hardly be understated. It is, first of all, difficult to believe that the Single Market could have been much of an advantage to its members, if their exports to the rest of the world were growing at a faster pace. More importantly, it also leads one to wonder whether a single market even exists in the sense of a market that may be distinguished from those beyond it, by the mobility of goods, capital, services and people guaranteed by its four freedoms, by the progressive harmonisation of rules, regulations and procedures within it, and by the mutual recognition of qualifications of service providers within it.

We have all come to believe that it exists, and that it is freer than, and offers greater opportunities to its members than, other markets, simply because so many EC officials talk and write about it a great deal, publish consultants' reports on its future, issue directives to enhance and enforce it, and sometimes even celebrate its achievements.[5] Successive British prime ministers have called for it to be extended and deepened, which rather implies that they have evidence of its existence. The doubts however, remain. If extra-EU services exports to idiosyncratically-regulated and distant markets have grown at a faster rate, one is bound to wonder what all this talk and paperwork amounts to. If it did exist, one would expect the growth of its members' exports to each other to show much less variance than their exports to the four corners of the world. But they don't.

One recent commentator, Wolfgang Munchau, after looking at the very slow rate of productivity during the Single Market, referred to it as 'a giant economic non-event, for both the EU and the UK'.[6] After looking at these figures, one is driven to the same conclusion about the 'single market' in services. In the present context, the vital point is that there is, as yet, no evidence to indicate that a single market in services has been of any advantage to its members. A recent investigation, The New City Initiative, a trade group of boutique fund managers, approaching the issue in a more hands-on manner, i.e. can we start our business in other member countries, came to a rather similar conclusion.[7]

We may, however, approach this question from another angle, by looking at the services exports of non-members to see if we can discern any disadvantages they may have faced.

## Growth of UK services exports to the EU versus six non-members

Although it is incomplete, uneven and belated (as of April 2015, the last complete year of data is 2012), the OECD database allows us to examine the growth of the services exports of a few non-member countries to members of the Single Market over the years 1999-2012, that is to say over 14 years rather than 11, since a number of non-members began to report services exports three years before most EU members, as did the UK which will therefore be the representative member country for comparative purposes. In terms of its export performance it is, as the data above indicates, far from the best candidate. In terms of the available data, it is the only candidate. However, we will return to this point later.

Before presenting the results, some of the limitations of the data and the difficulties facing any attempt to compile a matched set of countries for comparative purposes must be mentioned. There are five non-EU member countries with a reasonably complete, and reasonably uniform, set of data over very nearly the same number of years. They are Australia, Canada, Japan, Norway and the United States. To them we may add Hong Kong, since it also has a fairly full set of data reported by the OECD from 1999-2010 of its services exports to EU member countries. Since the only task here is to place the growth of UK services exports to fellow EU members alongside that of non-members in the hope of spotting the disadvantages of non-membership, there is no reason to limit the comparison to countries included in the earlier exercises. The more non-members the better.[8]

The data on these six countries to the EU do not, however, cover the same number of EU 'partner' countries. Ideally, there would be 14 partner countries, since there were 15 members of the Single Market in 1999, but in this analysis the UK is treated as an outsider, exporting to the EU alongside these six countries, and it cannot of course export to itself. We would therefore like to compare the six countries' exports to the other 14 with those of the UK to the same 14. We cannot do so. Norway has entries for 13 EU countries who were members pre-2000, Canada for 12, Hong Kong for 11, Japan and Australia for eight, and the US for only six. The reasons for these variations are unknown, and therefore one can only guess how this biases their returns. Presumably, countries which listed fewer of their EU export markets were more inclined to include the larger ones, though whether the larger are also growing faster or slower is a known unknown. However, we will deal with this problem in exactly the same way as we did when examining the EU data above; that is, by substituting 'imports from' for the missing 'exports to'. Hence, Australian exports to the EU consist of eight EU countries to which it reports its exports, plus imports from Australia reported by the six EU countries to which it has not reported its exports.

The number of years of data also varies. Australia and Canada have entries in the EBOPS (Extended Balance of Payments Services) 2002 classification up to 2008 and 2009 respectively, and were among the earliest to switch to the revised, and rather different, EBOPS 2010 classification, which OECD gives in a separate dataset. All the other countries including the UK still report in EBOPS 2002. After a less than convincing attempt to reconcile the two classifications, the EBOPS 2010 entries for the exports of Australia and Canada were ignored, and the graph therefore plots their growth only to 2008 and 2009 respectively. Hong Kong's stops in 2010, which was the last year reported, and there was nothing to be gained by making estimates for the last two years. Norway's exports for the years 1999-2001, and 2010 are also missing. The years 1999-2001 were estimated to give them the same starting point on the graph, by assuming that the proportion of Norway's world exports over these years going to EU members was the same as it was in the three following years 2002-2004. Its missing entry for 2010 was taken to be midway between those of 2009 and 2011. These estimates were, however, excluded from the calculations of Norway's CAGR, and the number of years included in the other CAGR calculations likewise varies with the years of real data available.

Figure 9 presents the results of these efforts to get a matched set of export destinations over the same number of years, and for the six countries. It shows the real growth of their services exports to EU member countries over the years 1999 to 2012, with a note below giving the specific details of each country so that the differences between them can be borne in mind before drawing any conclusions from the graph. The bracketed figure after the name of each country in the note is the number of EU partner countries for whom export data was available plus the number which relied on import data. The dollar figure is the peak pre-crisis value of their exports to the EU, in current value dollars. In the six countries this peak year is 2008, but for the UK it is, as may be seen, 2007. The percentage is the CAGR, in US (1999) dollars, in the value of each countries' exports over all the years of export data that were available for each of them between 1999 and 2012.

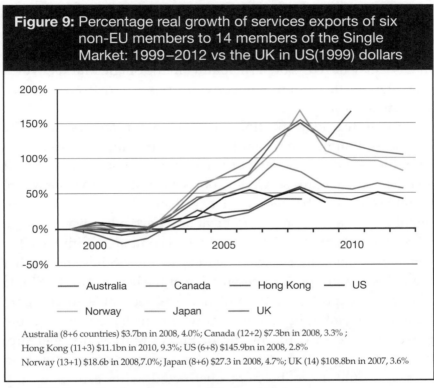

**Figure 9:** Percentage real growth of services exports of six non-EU members to 14 members of the Single Market: 1999–2012 vs the UK in US(1999) dollars

Australia (8+6 countries) $3.7bn in 2008, 4.0%; Canada (12+2) $7.3bn in 2008, 3.3% ;
Hong Kong (11+3) $11.1bn in 2010, 9.3%; US (6+8) $145.9bn in 2008, 2.8%
Norway (13+1) $18.6b in 2008,7.0%; Japan (8+6) $27.3 in 2008, 4.7%; UK (14) $108.8bn in 2007, 3.6%

Source: OECD Dataset: Trade in services, www.oecd.ilibrary.org/statistics )

On the face of things the export growth of the UK, the one country with all the advantages of EU membership, is not distinguished from that of the disadvantaged non-members in any meaningful way. It looks decidedly average. Three non-members have markedly higher growth, and three, including the largest exporter to the EU, the US, rather lower growth. Does the CAGR percentage point that separates the UK from the US show that the

UK has been reaping the advantages of membership, and/or the US has experienced the disadvantages of non-membership?

A great many other factors have affected the services exports of these countries over these years. We can say nothing about them, except that if they are to form a convincing case that membership of the Single Market has benefited UK services exports, they would have to be sufficient to show that were it not for its participation in the Single Market programme the growth of UK exports would have been lower. That sounds like a difficult task, and if we were to make a properly matched comparison we would have to allow for the costs of these UK exports to the UK taxpayer; that is to say the costs of participating in the Single Market, which taxpayers in these non-member countries, apart from Norway, altogether escape.

Pending the identification of these other factors, and the demonstration that they would overturn the impressions drawn from the raw data, we have little choice but to take the data as it stands, and chalk up services exports as another example where members cannot be shown to be at an advantage, and non-members cannot be shown to be at any particular disadvantage when exporting to the EU, at least when compared with the UK.

However, the data presented earlier in Table 8 has shown that the UK is a rather poor representative of the benefits of the Single Market on export growth, and had we been able to compare Ireland, Luxembourg or Portugal we might have made a more persuasive case for the merits of Single Market membership, though some questions would no doubt remain because missing entries would have been reconstructed with estimates and substitutes. There is, however, an alternative approach, and we will conclude by seeing how it may help the search for the benefits of the Single Market in services.

## Another view of the paradox

This alternative approach requires that we abandon export data altogether, and rely entirely on the import figures that we have intermittently used as a substitute for missing export figures. There are gains and losses in doing so. For some curious reason, import figures are often more complete than export data, and they have no omissions on grounds of confidentiality, but they begin at a later date. From 2004, they provide a complete return for the 35 OECD countries, and 28 non-members, and from 2006 for more than 150 more countries. In the present context, the file on the EU27 is particularly useful since it includes the 27 EU countries themselves as countries from which the EU27 has imported services alongside other OECD members and non-members. It thus provides a simple means of comparing the performance of EU members and non-members as exporters to the EU27, which cannot be done with the real export data.

All the countries from which the EU imported services, and whose file gave full details of their imports to the EU27 from 2004 to 2012 were eligible for inclusion, but to keep a manageable number they were subject to one filter: their imports were required to have a recorded total value of at least $1bn in the year 2012. In total 47 countries qualified, 23 of them EU members and 23 non-members. Table 9 presents the results, ranking the countries according to the CAGR of their exports, in 2004 US dollars, to the EU over the nine years to 2012. The value of their exports in 2012 is also given. EU member countries during the period are shaded.

If it were true that the Single Market had benefited the services exports of its members to each other, we would expect the member countries to figure disproportionately among the high growth exporters at the top of the ranking, and therefore to be disproportionately on the left hand side of the table. A slight tendency in that direction is visible, in that the top left quadrant of the table is more shaded than the top right quadrant, though it is also worth noting that countries in the top left quadrant are mainly 2004 EU entrants. Six of the 13 Single Market members on the left hand side are 2004 entrants and two are 2007 entrants, whereas nine of the 10 on the right hand side are founder members, and include all the larger EU economies – Germany, the UK, Italy, France and Spain – while the tenth, Austria, entered in 1995.

If we use the CAGR as a score of so many points, the EU member countries outscore the non-member countries. Their mean score is

**Table 9:** Growth of service exports of 47 EU member & non-member countries to 27 countries of the Single Market 2004-2012

As measured by reported imports to the 27 EU countries ranked in order of compound annual growth rate. EU member countries during the period are shaded.

| | CAGR % (in 2004 US$) | 2012 value (in 2012 US$bn) | | CAGR % (in 2004 US$) | 2012 value (in 2012 US$bn) |
|---|---|---|---|---|---|
| China | 11.01 | 21.1 | **Continued** | | |
| Slovak Rep. | 10.93 | 6.8 | Israel* | 4.19 | 3.5 |
| India | 10.51 | 11.3 | Australia | 3.72 | 8.6 |
| Estonia | 9.96 | 2.5 | Germany | 3.65 | 115.5 |
| Ireland | 9.85 | 35.1 | Denmark | 3.10 | 16.8 |
| Singapore | 9.25 | 12.8 | Canada | 2.81 | 10.8 |
| Romania | 9.07 | 5.9 | Japan | 2.61 | 16.4 |
| Luxemb'g | 8.89 | 26.9 | Korea* | 2.56 | 5.0 |
| Poland | 8.87 | 18.7 | Turkey* | 2.44 | 15.1 |
| Bulgaria | 8.21 | 4.0 | UK | 2.32 | 114.2 |
| Chile* | 6.45 | 1.7 | US | 2.10 | 159.2 |
| Argentina | 6.36 | 2.4 | NZ | 1.50 | 1.6 |
| Slovenia | 6.32 | 2.9 | Egypt* | 1.48 | 5.9 |
| Russian Fed. | 6.12 | 15.9 | Belgium | 1.44 | 38.1 |
| Netherlands | 5.74 | 75.2 | Portugal | 1.34 | 10.6 |
| Czech Rep | 5.73 | 12.9 | Italy | 1.31 | 48.4 |
| Hungary | 5.65 | 9.0 | Norway* | 1.16 | 13.0 |
| Switzerland* | 5.60 | 64.2 | Austria | 0.99 | 29.9 |
| Sweden | 5.49 | 24.6 | France | 0.84 | 83.4 |
| Nigeria | 5.29 | 2.1 | Iceland* | 0.74 | 0.8 |
| Indonesia | 5.24 | 2.0 | Spain | 0.35 | 54.4 |
| Croatia** | 4.88 | 6.3 | Mexico* | 0.07 | 3.4 |
| Finland | 4.77 | 9.4 | S. Africa* | -0.19 | 4.8 |
| Hong Kong | 4.42 | 9.2 | Greece | -2.18 | 13.7 |

*Indicates countries with which the EU had a trade agreement in force at some point in these years

** Became a member of the EU in 2014

The selection filter means Lithuania, Latvia, Cyprus and Malta are not featured on the table.

Sources: OECD Dataset: EBOPS 2002 – Trade in Services by Partner Country European Union (27 countries) Total Services Imports

4.5 versus non-members' 3.9, though it should be remembered that the EU countries enjoy an advantage over non-members that is known to be a decisive determinant of trade growth, and has absolutely nothing to do with the EU: geographical propinquity.

A two-sample, two-tailed t test shows that there is no significant difference between the mean growth rates (p=0.473). A Mann-Whitney non-parametric test on the rankings (unpaired, with two samples) agrees. There is only a 55 per cent probability that export growth from a random EU country will exceed that from a random non-EU country. The fact that even with their in-built geographical advantage, the growth of EU members' exports to each other cannot be distinguished from that of non-members is an important finding, leading one to wonder once again whether a single market in services actually exists.

If one sets the initial admission filter higher, and compares only those economies with exports of at least $10bn in 2012, we are left to compare 16 member countries with 10 non-member countries. The mean CAGR of the members was 3.6 per cent and that of the non-members was 5.3 per cent. Amongst high value exporters therefore, it is the non-members that have appear to have grown faster. However, this difference is not significant either. The two-tailed t test has a p-value of 0.24, and the non-parametric test gives only a 66 per cent probability that the growth of the exports of a random non-EU member will exceed a random EU member. This suggests that there are many more important determinants of the rate of growth of services exports to the EU than the advantages or disadvantages of membership. In all probability, we will only discover what they may be if services are disaggregated.

For the moment, we may simply note that the growth of non-members' services exports to the EU has not outpaced that of members, and so they are not, by this statistical measure, a paradox to the same degree as goods exports. However, since member countries have enjoyed the massive, inherent, and oft-demonstrated advantage of geographical propinquity, and since some of them must pay considerable sums to remain members of the Single Market, and also accept free movement of people, and other limitations of their sovereignty, there cannot be much doubt that, in value-for-money terms, they have been outperformed by non-members. Services are therefore another example of the paradox: non-members out-perform members. They have been the main beneficiaries of the Single Market.

# 6

## Does 'helping to make the rules' in Brussels help UK exports?

The idea that there is no evidence to show that the Single Market has benefited UK goods and services exports to other members will be disconcerting to a lot of good minds and good people in Britain who have long assumed that there is. Political leaders of all three main parties have repeatedly told them of the Single Market's significant economic benefits and they assume, even in an era of profound distrust of political leaders, that these would not all make the same claim, unless some authoritative agency or person had actually measured these benefits, and confirmed that their claim was correct.

The further conclusion that the exports of many non-members to the Single Market have grown more rapidly than those of the UK, so that they might reasonably be said to have been its prime beneficiaries, will be doubly disconcerting. The benefits for UK exports were supposed to be a return for all the political and economic costs of membership of the EU that those same good people have been obliged to pay, at the behest of these same political leaders. The idea that non-member countries which have contributed nothing to those costs have enjoyed even greater benefits, and that the growth of their exports has exceeded those of members, especially the UK, is bound to be rather galling. Moreover, it flies in the face both of received economic wisdom, and even of common sense. For 40 years the EU has been engaged in removing barriers to trade in goods and services between its members, so their exports to each other over these years must, one may reasonably presume, have increased rather more than those of non-members who faced these barriers all the while. It makes no sense that they have not.

It is possible, of course, that there were a range of favourable conditions in non-members' labour markets, in foreign exchange or commodity markets, in technology and the like, which improved their relative comparative advantages, and more or less simultaneously enabled them to overcome the disadvantages of non-membership. It is also possible that, over these same years, all or most of the member countries happened to encounter adverse circumstances that cancelled out their membership advantages. The disadvantages of non-members and the advantages of members may, in other words, exist, but cannot be observed in raw trade data owing to the intervention of extraneous factors that have nothing to do with the Single Market.

Until such time as these extraneous factors are identified, and their contribution to the export performances of non-member and member countries demonstrated, we have to confront the evidence that has been accumulating over several years and is available to anyone who cares to examine it. There are no doubt individual UK companies, and perhaps entire industrial sectors, whose exports to other EU members have benefited from the Single Market, and can be seen and shown to have benefited by comparison both with previous decades and with non-member competitors.[1] However, we are here considering UK export of goods and services as a whole, and there is no evidence that they have benefited from membership of the Single Market. If we are unwilling to recognise this surprising and disconcerting fact, it is difficult to see how the paradox will ever be understood, explained or resolved. And if it is not resolved, it is difficult to see how UK governments could adopt sensible policies towards the EU, or how the UK electorate could ever make an informed choice about the merits of EU membership.

## The public good aspect of EU rules

The EC staff who stumbled upon the first signs of this paradox in 2007, looking at 2003 data, did not want to make much of it, observing nonchalantly that:

> ...extra-EU exporters have also benefited from the suppression of intra-EU trade barriers and from the application of the principle of mutual recognition. In manufacturing since 1988 and until 2003 (latest available data) the share of extra EU suppliers... has gradually increased at the expense of domestic production.

However, they affected no particular interest or concern in this shift, merely observing that:

> ...the slowdown of trade growth within the EU15 and euro-zone relative to trade growth with third partners is unsurprising given the already very intense trade flows within the EU15 and the large untapped opportunities for trade gains with third partners.[2]

It is a neat and happy solution to the puzzle: intra-EU trade has been so intense and successful that a slowdown is to be expected, leaving large untapped opportunities for non-members. Perhaps for members of the commission this solution was persuasive, and even for some member countries. For the UK it is less so, since their trade or at least their exports to the EU have not been 'very intense', and their performance has remained inferior to that of a large number of disadvantaged non-members over many years. For UK observers at least, the paradox deserves much more attention than the EC staff cared to give it eight years ago.

In 2006 two Swedish economists, Harry F Flam and Håkan Nordström, came across a somewhat similar paradox when examining the early impact of the euro on trade. Like membership of the EU and the Single Market programme, the euro was intended to increase trade amongst its members, and its supporters warned the UK and other sceptical countries of dire consequences for their trade within the EU if they chose to remain outside it. In the event, Flam and Nordström, working with limited data from the first four years of the euro, 1999-2002, found that 'contrary to our expectations, exports to the euro countries are increased to the same extent as exports from euro countries'.[3] They went on to describe this as a 'spillover' effect, and attributed it to increased vertical specialisation in manufacturing across national borders of eurozone and non-euro countries in Europe. In their view, producers outside the eurozone are 'able to purchase cheaper inputs from the euro countries, which makes them more competitive and can increase their exports back to the euro countries'. Unfortunately, they had no data to support this comforting hypothesis.

Their paper was, however, reviewed sympathetically by Richard Baldwin, and his work prompted reports in two UK publications that had once enthusiastically supported UK membership of the currency.[4] In an article in June 2006 entitled 'The supposed benefits of monetary union are cut down to size', *The Economist* noted that previous estimates (of the likely trade effect of the euro) are 'fatally flawed'. It repeated Baldwin's estimate that the boost to trade from joining the euro was a one-off nine per cent, but that Britain, Sweden and Denmark have boosted their trade to the eurozone by seven per cent over the same period.[5] The *Financial Times* posed the question 'Has Britain been the clever one staying out of the euro?' It also noted that 'adoption of the euro has boosted imports from non-euro area nations almost as much as imports from eurozone countries', and concluded that 'for policy-makers, the implication is that adopting the euro would have only a small effect on the joiner's exports, but that imports should rise substantially more than exports'.[6] In other words, which the FT did not use, 'joining the euro, as we strongly advised, would probably have been disastrous for the UK, given its chronic balance of payments deficit'.

In recent years, analysis of the benefits of the euro for non-members has understandably been overshadowed by analysis of its demerits for some of its own members. In a study of a much-publicised model predicting a vast growth in intra-EU trade as a result of the adoption of the new currency, the growth in exports of goods of 10 eurozone countries to each other was *inter alia* compared with that of six European non-euro countries to them, up to 2011. It showed there is little to choose between them. Indeed, if the largest exporter of the non-euro six, the UK, is excluded, the growth of non-euro countries has been strikingly *more* rapid than that of the Eurozone countries, which makes the 'spillover' effect, if that is what is at work, a still more remarkable phenomenon. Outsiders, or five of them at least, have not just benefited from the euro, they have benefited even more than insiders.[7]

It does not seem likely that Flam and Nordström's 'spillover' hypothesis will help to explain the larger Single Market paradox of why exports of goods from non-member countries around the world to the EU have grown more during the first two decades of the Single Market than those of its own members. Nor will it explain why, for all the attempts to create a Single Market in services, the growth of services exports to the EU from countries scattered around the world equal, and sometimes surpass, those of neighbours and fellow members of the programme.

The resolution of this paradox will require intensive research and analysis far beyond the present review of currently available evidence. However, one contributory factor that might help to explain it deserves a brief word, even though it will probably have occurred to anyone who paid attention during Economics 101. Whatever else they may be, the rules of the Single Market are, in many respects, a public good. Those sitting round the table may intend to help only themselves but, irrespective of their intentions, by imposing uniform rules and standards on each other, they also necessarily if inadvertently help those who have taken no part in devising them. They allow exporters in independent countries to comply with just one set of technical or SPS standards, and with only one set of administrative and customs procedures when exporting to members of the EU, instead of 28, and therefore reduce the trade costs of non-members.

In all probability, the current TTIP negotiations between the US and the EU will have similar benefits for exporters around the world who are taking no part in them. American tariffs are already low, and any benefits exclusively for EU members from their further reduction are likely to be of marginal significance, other than a few specific sectors. Much the greater gains for future trade are expected to flow from the lowering or removal of NTBs, and in particular from the harmonisation of the differing technical (TBT) and sanitary and phytosanitary (SPS) regulations of the US and the EU. Any progress in this direction will necessarily, and unavoidably, benefit exporters of third countries just as much as those from the US and the EU. If the UK were to leave the EU, therefore, it would still be a major beneficiary of TTIP if and when it comes into force.

## The web of global and national and EU rules

Before deciding whether there is any merit in the argument of many British political leaders that the UK benefits by 'sitting around the table and helping to make the rules' of the Single Market, and that UK exporters would lose greatly if it no longer did so, we have first to pause and ask what kind of rules we are talking about, since some rules offer members no advantage, and put non-members at no disadvantage. The British wrote the rules of football, rugby, cricket, golf and many other sports, but few around the world who play these games know or care about their origin, and no one surely believes that this gives the British any particular advantage when playing them.

The Single Market has many such mandatory rules and standards for the conduct of trade and their source or authorship is of no particular concern to exporters anywhere. In fact, many of these rules and standards are not made by the EU at all, but by international bodies which the EU has merely imported and imposed, both on its own members as well as on third country exporters who wish to sell in the Single Market.[8] They cannot therefore offer any particular advantage to members who helped to 'make' them or transpose them, or be of any particular disadvantage to non-members who did not. Indeed, some of them may well put Single Market members at a disadvantage, since manufacturers in non-member countries, other than those who wish to export to the EU, have a choice of whether or not to adopt them, whereas EU rules apply to all manufacturers in member countries whether or not they export to other members.

These trade rules are but one strand in the complex web of rules that surrounds economic activity in the EU. Members of the Single Market are subject to a second kind of rule which applies only to them, and to members of the EEA. These membership rules are mainly intended to ensure a level playing field within the Single

Market, either to promote the solidarity and ever-closer union of its members, or to further various social and environmental goals akin to, though more stringent than, the social and environmental pillars of EU-FTAs discussed above. The Working Time Directive has become the flagship example of such membership rules, which are far more onerous and intrusive than mere trade rules, and far more costly. There might perhaps be some advantage for members helping to make these rules, since they might make them rather less costly for their exporters, but overall they must be a decided and costly disadvantage, and a considerable comparative advantage to exporters in non-member third countries who are not subject to them.

Imperceptibly, however, these membership rules to create a level playing field by harmonizing rules, practices and institutions within the Single Market may merge into a third type of rule which also applies only to member countries and excludes non-members. The conspicuous current example is the attempt to create a union-wide system of financial regulation, but this kind of exclusionary rule-making might sometime in the future be applied to all regulated service industries, such as telecoms, media, air, rail and sea transport, media and couriers, which are a very large swathe of any modern economy. Sitting around the table and helping to make these rules at some time in the future would be a clear advantage to producers in member countries and if and when regulation morphs into protection a very clear disadvantage to non-members. The WTO and OECD have recently come to recognise that this is what such regulation often does, and have taken steps to identify these covert forms of protection, and to campaign against them.

Beneath these EU trade and membership rules, national rules of member states, which usually long preceded the EU, remain in place in most services industries. They differ widely, as the Services Trade Restrictiveness Index (STRI) recently created by the OECD amply testifies.[9] No doubt the EC would one day like to harmonise and/or replace them all, in the manner of the proposed unified financial regulation. That however is in the distant future, and at present, and for the foreseeable future, national rules apply.

The interesting and uncertain question about them is whether fellow EU member countries enjoy any decisive advantages over their non-member competitors when facing fellow members' national rules.

In principle, service providers from other member countries have two clear advantages. If there are nationality requirements, and there usually are in regulated services, providers from any member countries satisfy them *ipso facto*. A second advantage is that when formal qualifications are required as they are in many services, mandatory mutual recognition of the qualifications within the EU means they cannot be used against providers from another member state to restrict access.

In practice however, these do not appear to be particularly telling advantages. Non-member countries willing to negotiate *ad hoc* reciprocity agreements can easily match them. Many other rules restricting access to the provision of services such as registration and residential rules, advertising, fee-setting and splitting, and company formation and structure rules, are of course primarily intended to restrict access *within* each member state by their own citizens.

In practice, providers from other member states and from non-member states seem to be treated as equally foreign and are about equally well, or equally poorly, placed to surmount the national rules of member countries. Neither of the studies of the rules facing foreign service providers, one commissioned by the EC and the other by the OECD, bothered to distinguish between fellow EU members and non-members since both were treated in most cases as equally foreign.[11] Both are of course equally placed to surmount one of the most significant and non-negotiable restrictions on services trade: language.

The picture painted of sitting round the table and helping to make the rules can therefore be a rather misleading one. It implies that these rules are making life easier for traders in member countries, and rather more difficult, in a discreet WTO-compliant manner, for traders in non-member countries. In the event, many of the rules are of no particular advantage to those who make them, or import them. Others are a positive disadvantage to members, and no sensible non-member would dream of sitting around the table, helping to make them, and then going back home to impose the costs they entail on their exporters and everyone else. Thus the main benefit of sitting round the table, in the UK case, is reduced to preventing regulatory rules becoming a covert form of protection. Whenever a member country is successful in this respect, it can hardly be said to be acting to the disadvantage of non-members.

In the background of most discussions about EU membership is a mental balance-sheet of the trade advantages and disadvantages of EU membership and rules. For defenders of continued membership, both sides of this balance sheet, both goods and services, are high: advantages are considerable assets and disadvantages significant potential liabilities. Indeed, it is by no means uncommon, to find stout defenders of membership who warn that non-membership would mean a drastic curtailment of UK trade with its neighbours. All the available evidence we have considered above is impossible to reconcile with this image, since it repeatedly suggests that both the advantages of membership and disadvantages of non-membership have been modest, especially the latter. If non-members have been facing severe disadvantages, how is it possible that the growth of the exports of so many of them has surpassed that of members? And how, likewise, if the advantages of membership were so great could so many members, especially the UK, fail to benefit from them?

Plainly we need to replace this imaginary balance sheet with a real one, and that will require a careful and regular audit of the trade costs of members and non-members doing business within the Single Market, both for goods and services, preferably over time. There are a number of precedents of tariff equivalent costs.[12] The trade costs of members ought of course to include all the costs that trade within the Single Market entails, and this raises a tricky methodological issue. One of its peculiarities is that in place of a tariff on trade with its other members, the EU imposes annual subscription charges on its members, or at least on its wealthier members. However this tariff-substitute does not figure in the trade costs of exporters, since payment of it is distributed across the population at large, on non-exporting companies and on all taxpayers. Thus this audit has to be ready to capture this difference, and also be prepared for other surprises. As noted earlier, despite the removal of tariffs on goods before the Single Market came into existence, a report in 2011 found 'huge variation in the costs of trading [of goods] across EU member states', long after a common regulatory framework of the Single Market in goods was thought to have come into existence.[13] But they must also be prepared to recognise the unthinkable: that the trade costs of members trading with each other are as high, or higher, than those of non-members.

However, the main difficulty for such research is not tricky methodological issues or collecting the data, but overcoming the initial reluctance to believe that it is necessary at all. The myth that the Single Market has delivered 'significant economic benefits' to Britain is so pervasive, has been repeated by so many political leaders, on so many occasions, has been shared for so long by great swathes of the UK media, that it is treated as a self-evident truth that requires no empirical verification whatever. Over 40 and more years no British government has ever sought to regularly collect evidence about the impact of EU membership on UK exports, and there were therefore no British sources worth citing in the research reported in this paper. When so much faith has been invested in the EU project, and when the careers and reputations of so many politicians have been staked on it, the idea that research should be conducted to discover and measure the exact advantages of membership and the disadvantages of non-membership is bound to be considered unnecessary and to be strongly resisted.

# Part Three

## Conclusions

# 7

# Image without substance

Joseph Schumpeter once observed: 'The first thing a man will do for his ideal is lie.' He might have added that, short of lying, men (and women) will also exaggerate for it, lower or forget their critical standards when discussing it, and overlook evidence that conflicts with it. And since they are inclined to mix with those who share their ideal, they will tend to reassure one another, and convert their shared hopes, predictions and impressions into established facts. And if, by chance, one of them happens to lie and mislead when discussing it, the rest will courteously ignore their fellow believer's slip, on the grounds that their shared ideal itself is such a worthy one. So it has been with the Single Market.

Perhaps we should not be too surprised therefore that when a committed pro-EU minister made fanciful, even fantastic, claims to a parliamentary committee, its members let them pass without a murmur. They were, after all, only confirming their support for an image of the Single Market that has been shared by most of the political and business elite of the UK for a long time before these hearings. Almost everyone seems to have been persuaded that this Single Market is no more than an extension of the principles of free trade that we all accept. Necessarily, therefore, it must have been a successful project, in need of further refinement perhaps, or as the minister put it 'modernisation', but definitely not requiring close scrutiny and evaluation. It is this pervasive and enduring image, and its extraordinary indifference to evidence, that deserves our attention rather than one minister's exuberant reaffirmation of it.

Kenneth Clarke, a former chancellor, has in recent years become a media favourite for enthusiastic pro-EU soundbites. In 2013, however, he decided 'to put the European case more strongly'. He did so by declaring: 'The benefits we reap from it are quite astonishing.'[1] Perhaps more than most I was ready to be astonished, but alas, he declined to identify a single one of these benefits. One of Sir John Major's constant themes in his annual conference and after dinner speeches is that FDI in the UK is dependent on membership of the Single Market, even though the EC itself, as we have seen, decided in 2007 that 'the internal market has not been able to deliver in terms of promoting further the role of the EU with respect to global investment flows.' Sir John seems completely unfazed by this and other research on the subject that repeatedly contradicts him.[2]

In a speech to the British Chambers of Commerce in April 2014, Lord Mandelson, a former EU trade commissioner, argued that the Single Market brought great benefits to UK trade which would be lost if we were to leave. He thought that 'it made no sense to exit a market on Britain's doorstop and a move in that direction would erode the country's ability to trade with others… India would laugh in our faces if Britain tried to negotiate a free trade agreement outside Europe… They would walk away and leave us whistling in the wind.'[3] But he declined to explain why India did not leave Singapore or Chile 'whistling in the wind', or why leaving the EU would require the UK to exit the market on its doorstep. Switzerland obviously has not exited the market on its doorstep, and it has negotiated FTAs more rapidly than the EU, with larger economies, and they more frequently include services.

Lord Mandelson must, one imagines, have been told all these things *ex officio*. He served for about a year as secretary of state for trade and industry, before becoming EU trade commissioner, after which he became UK business secretary. In all of these positions, he was ideally placed to initiate and reflect on research on the Single Market's contribution to the British economy. His British ministerial offices, one would have thought, required such information simply to enable him to perform his official duties effectively. And one imagines that an EU trade commissioner would have to know whether EC-negotiated FTAs were effective or not, and how they compared with those of other countries.

Apparently, he did not think so, and left one of his successors to begin the long overdue task of evaluating their merits.[4]

While he may be the most striking case, the other political leaders also let pass their opportunity to contribute evidence to the debate about EU membership. As chancellor, Mr Clarke could surely have itemised a few of the 'astonishing benefits' of EU membership, and as prime minister, Sir John Major could have asked for a study of FDI in the UK to see how far it depended on EU membership. They all seem to have let their opportunity slip, and so their arguments out of office depend entirely on the lingering authority of the high offices they once held rather than research and evidence.

Unfortunately, the frequent repetition of these views is seldom challenged by the media who report them, with demands to know the evidence on which they are based, and perhaps citing evidence that contradicts them. This surely is one of the nobler missions of journals of opinion in a free society, but in the case of the EU many journalists also seem to think that evidence about its economic benefits is now superfluous, and hence evidence-based debate which their intervention might have provoked, never begins.

A leader writer for *The Times* provides one recent example. He argued that the UK should remain in the EU because of 'the gains of belonging to a large consumer market'. He then claimed that 'there's no cost-free way of gaining access to the internal market', wholly indifferent to the published sources which have shown over many recent years that the goods and services exports of a large number of countries who do not 'belong' to the Single Market, and do not pay any costs for access to it, have increased at a faster rate than those of the UK and many other member countries.[5]

A former *Financial Times* journalist is another example. He made a case for remaining a member, in which he portrayed the Single Market as the EU's 'crown jewel'. If that were so, he would, with all the resources and experts of the *FT* on call, have been spoilt for choice for evidence to demonstrate some of the facets of this crown jewel. However, he chose not to cite any contemporary evidence from Eurostat, or the OECD, or UNCTAD or any other authoritative database, and instead rested his case on a 2008 analysis of six steps in the process of European integration followed by rough estimates of their economic consequences.[6] For a journalist long accustomed, as a former editor of the Lex column, to taking a sceptical view of events and decisions in the City of London this is surely very curious behaviour. Would estimates of the past performance of a company without reference to its current accounts have persuaded him to warmly commend it to his readers? Different standards evidently apply when discussing the EU.

As we have seen in the submissions to the Foreign Office, the business elite also seem to have similar double standards. If they themselves are trading reasonably successfully within the EU, they seem to think that this entitles them to speak out confidently on questions of public policy towards the EU without the help of the kind of research they expect before taking major decisions within their own companies. On the basis of their submissions, it is a fair bet that neither they, nor any of their trade federations, had the least idea about Swiss or Singaporean FTAs, or are aware that the US has 13 FTAs currently in force, with 20 countries, and that all 20 are with countries smaller than the UK.[7] If they had, would they confidently claim that the EU's 'collective clout' and 'negotiating leverage' are essential when negotiating with larger powers? Did any of them, one wonders, reflect on the fact that the most significant EC agreements, in terms of post-agreement UK export growth over the 40 years up to 2012, have been with Syria, Lebanon and Tunisia.[8] Did they ask themselves why it is that exports of goods from so many non-member countries to the EU have grown so much faster than those of the UK? Or why it has proved so difficult for the EC to include services in its FTAs, while those of many independent countries have often managed to do so?

Perhaps it is unfair to expect individual companies to address such questions. Their eyes are focused, naturally enough, on their own bottom lines. Trade federations might perhaps have done so, especially the CBI since it presents itself as the voice of British business, but at the end of the day these are national questions, affecting the British economy as a whole and the livelihoods and wellbeing of the British people as a whole. As such, they are properly the concern of the British government. But it too has failed to ask these questions, let alone answer them. Over more than 40 years, no UK government has sought to monitor the performance of UK trade within the EU, or to assign any government department the task of collecting, analysing and publishing, on a regular basis, evidence about its growth relative to that of non-members, or to trade with the rest of the world. This looks like a careless disregard of one of their primary duties towards the people of Britain. Even on so basic a matter as the costs of the entire project, voters have been obliged to depend on the voluntary, private effort of Gerard Batten and Tim Congdon, 'How much does the European Union cost Britain?' Its seventh edition in 2014 remains the most conscientious, reliable and comprehensive analysis of the cost of the EU to the UK published to date.[9] But isn't their research properly the business of government?

Since governments have not been reluctant to collect, analyse and publish evidence about most kinds of domestic public expenditure, other than the security services, their indifference – if that is what it is – with respect to the EU requires some explanation. In part, it may be one further consequence of the oft-noted democratic deficit of the EU. There are, in the case of EC expenditures, no robust equivalents to the kinds of media, NGO and public pressures which force UK governments to explain and account for their domestic expenditures. One of the odder facts that emerged during this investigation was that the minister who provoked it had to rely on evidence and arguments supplied by the EC, rather than that collected by his own department.[10] UK governments have evidently taken the view that their responsibility to the UK taxpayer ends after they hand over their money to meet the UK share of EU expenditures of the EC. Thereafter the EC is alone responsible for seeing that it is wisely spent, and the UK government is not required to hold it accountable.

A more important reason for this governmental indifference is that, from the very beginning, British politicians committed to the EU have seen themselves more as advocates of the project, than as representatives of the British people, whose duty it is to see that British taxpayers' contributions to the project are spent wisely. They have been obliged to become advocates since they have never been able to forget that a considerable proportion of the British people are uneasy about the surrender of sovereignty and of executive power over them to agencies, institutions and people who may be formally and circuitously accountable to them, but in practice are neither accountable, nor even for the most part even identifiable.

It is no surprise that the British are more uneasy about this transfer of power than the peoples of other member countries. The history and character of the British people is largely defined by their centuries-long struggles to restrain and limit the executive power of the state, to subject it to the rule of law, and to render it accountable to them. Their early success in these struggles (which are far from over as the debate on EU membership indicates) long distinguished them from most other member countries, so the idea of ceding state powers to a supra-national executive body, supported by a supra-national court committed to increasing the power of that executive, is bound to be rather more disturbing and offensive to them than it is to the peoples of most other member countries.

As a result, the political elite who started this transfer of state power to the European Community in the 1960s and 1970s, and their successors who have wanted to maintain and continue it, have been more or less continuously engaged in persuading the British people, who have never expressed the least wish for any kind of supra-national government or for political union with their neighbours, that the EU is beneficial, inoffensive and even inevitable. And they have decided that the best way of persuading them is to downplay the political implications as much as possible, and to concentrate on the economic benefits of membership, and the promise of many more in the future.

Unfortunately these benefits have proved remarkably difficult to identify, as all the data presented above only confirms. The leading enthusiasts for EU membership, both past and present, have therefore been obliged to describe these benefits in simple, vacuous and undeniable truisms. Thus, they have frequently observed UK exports a lot to its fellow members, that exports to them have increased, and that many British jobs depend on these exports. This simple message can hardly be disproved since every country in the world exports a lot to their nearest neighbours, and have increased and, yes, British jobs do depend on these exports.[11] They never feel any need to complicate their simple message by pointing out that the UK also traded a lot with them in 1972, or 1872 for that matter, or that UK exports to non-members in Europe have increased faster than those to the EU, or that the exports of many non-members to the EU have grown much faster than those of the UK. Their simple message is sometimes reinforced by the fearful prospect that the exports to the EU and the jobs that depend on them are threatened, and might even end altogether, if the UK were to leave the EU. Since it only says what might happen, this too is a claim that cannot be readily disproved. Pigs might, after all, fly.

Identifying and measuring the problems, disappointments and varying fortunes of the Single Market along the way, as the EC staff were willing to do in 2007, and then introducing these into public debate in the UK is evidently not an option, presumably because it is thought that such research would do little but undermine their case for continued membership. A few flaws in the project may be readily admitted, such as excessive regulation by the EU, or inadequate coverage of services in its Single Market, but these are pardonable, temporary and negotiable, and indeed, these acknowledged flaws can be readily converted into arguments for continued membership. The main aim of governments over all these years has been to ensure that membership of the EU is seen as a remarkable achievement, a prized asset, which the UK must not on any account abandon or let slip from its grasp. This has resulted in a mis-selling of the trade benefits of the Single Market comparable in some respects to the mis-selling of payment protection insurance (PPI), though on a larger scale, over a longer period, and with far more serious consequences. PPI offered borrowers protection that on closer inspection proved to be illusory, and at disproportionate cost. The evidence above shows that the same might well be said of the Single Market.

Once one recognises that the UK political elite has long been engaged on a mission of persuading the British people to accept a project of which they are temperamentally suspicious and sceptical, their reluctance to collect and publish reliable and impartial research seems less like indifference, or a careless disregard for the interests of the British people, and more like a deliberate strategy. The refusal of the recent Labour governments to initiate an authoritative cost/benefit analysis of EU membership called for by Lord Pearson in 2006, 2009 and 2010, a call which the Coalition also ignored, is a pretty clear indication that past governments were not merely forgetful, but did not wish to collect and present evidence, some of which might show the EU in a less than favourable light. It is a strategy that may well have helped the EU cause in the UK, but it has done no service at all to the Single Market project whose problems are not identified and addressed, and therefore remain unresolved.

In 2013 the Treasury published two impressive volumes on public policy, the so-called Green and Magenta Books.[12] They start from the principle that public policy should be 'based on reliable and robust evidence', and that 'high quality evaluation is vital to this'. Together they 'provide detailed guidelines... on how policies and projects should be assessed and reviewed... the Green Book emphasising the economic principles that should be applied to both appraisal and evaluation, and the Magenta Book providing in-depth guidance on how evaluation should be designed and undertaken'. They are outstanding works in the methodology of public policy, especially the Magenta volume, but perhaps the most remarkable thing about them is that no government has ever asked that their methods be applied to the biggest, lifelong UK public project of them all, the EU.

If the Treasury had insisted that policy towards the EU had been evaluated in the manner suggested in the Green and Magenta Books, the OECD, UN Comtrade, Eurostat and other trade databases would have been routinely monitored and analysed, all the distinctive problems of the Single Market documented here and elsewhere would have been part of the public debate about the merits of the Single Market and of continued membership of the EU.

All the questions raised in this search would by now have been examined and probably answered. We would already know, for instance, whether it is unreasonable to expect UK exports to other members to have grown as fast as they did in Common Market decades and why they didn't. We would already know the added costs, and the scale of the subsidy to UK companies exporting to the Single Market, and why they have nevertheless only managed a rather slow rate of growth compared with the exports of many unsubsidised non-member countries. Most important of all, we would already have devised reliable measures of the progress of the Single Market in services, and whether it has grown as slowly as the commission's own measure suggests, and what the reasons for this might be. In short, we would now be able to rest assured that UK government's policy towards the EU has been, and is, 'based on reliable and robust evidence'. Currently, we have no such assurance.

The remarks by the current prime minister provide none. In what was publicised as a keynote speech on the EU at Bloomberg's London headquarters in 2013, setting out his intended policy towards the EU over future years, he observed: 'Our participation in the Single Market, and our ability to help set its rules, is the principal reason for our membership of the EU.'[13] Given that, after helping to set the rules, UK exports to the EU have not grown as fast as they did under the Common Market, nor as much as exports of 27 non-member countries to members of the Single Market, one can only assume that he thinks that sitting at the table and helping to set its rules is, in and of itself, the principal reason for our membership of the EU, regardless of its results. Either that, or the prime minister has not the least idea of what the results of helping to set the rules have been for UK exports.

On balance, the latter seems the more likely. The inadequate, dated and irrelevant evidence available to the minister who was responsible for co-ordinating EU policy in the Department for Business, Innovation and Skills has been examined above, and there is no reason to think that the evidence collected by the Treasury over the years has been of a higher quality. Since these are the two government departments that are most concerned with monitoring and understanding the impact of the EU on the UK trade, it would seem the prime minister is as ignorant as his former minister and the rest of us. How could he or anyone else know anything about the matter, other than what he has been told by the EC, or by a media sympathetic to the project?

We are all – prime ministers, ministers, civil servants, journalists, media interviewers and voters alike – in the same boat, profoundly ignorant of the economic consequences of the EU, and of the Single Market, for UK trade. We are all involved in, and for the time being at least committed to, a project or a programme that none of us know much about, sailing along in our own British-made ship of fools, with an upper deck steadfastly refusing to prepare and consult reliable charts, and old salts doing their best to reassure crew and passengers that all is for the best.

Given that the prime minister intends to renegotiate the terms of UK membership of the EU project, and then to hold a referendum on them, this is rather disconcerting. How could he negotiate effectively on behalf of the British people if he does not know exactly what the adverse effects have been, and what benefits are worth defending? If, for instance, he actually believed that the UK has gained by sitting at the table, and that the Single Market is indeed 'a crown jewel', and other members knew that he considered it as such, it is difficult to see why they should concede anything at all. If, on the other hand, he was aware that non-members trade more successfully with the Single Market than the UK, then he need have little hesitation in walking away. More to the point, other members would know that he will not hesitate to walk away, and be more likely therefore to accede to his proposals.

The same might be said of all the other familiar arguments for remaining a member of the EU. If Sir John Major persuaded him that FDI in the UK really depended on membership of the Single Market, or if Lord Mandelson persuaded him that independently-negotiated FTAs were bound to fail, or if his former deputy Nick Clegg persuaded him that the Single Market, despite having been a region of chronically and distinctively high unemployment since it began, is nevertheless good for jobs in the UK, and if other EU members with whom he was negotiating knew that he shared these views, the chances of them accepting any of his proposals seem slim. Strictly from a negotiating point of view, the prime minister is in a curious position. Those who present themselves as his friends and allies are of no help whatever, while his eurosceptic enemies, especially those armed with reliable evidence that the EU has brought less than astonishing benefits to the UK, are his strongest allies. The large number of UKIP representatives in the European Parliament are of course also his allies, probably his most important ones. Without them, his renegotiation would already be a certain failure.

If his renegotiations were to result in some meaningful and tangible alterations in the terms of membership, the referendum will raise its own problems. If the UK government remains as ill-informed as the business minister was in 2010, or as inaccurate and misleading as his secretary of state was in 2014, or as superficial and prejudiced as Treasury research papers have been over many years, we may expect the worst: little more than a re-run of the flawed 1975 referendum. In 1975, however, no one had any experience of conducting a referendum, and nobody could be particularly well-informed on the issues since the EU project had barely begun.

The forthcoming referendum should and could be on a quite different level, since we have the example of the inadequacies of the 1975 and other referendums in mind, and the electorate will have more than 40 years of experience and evidence upon which to base their vote. However, unless that experience is documented, analysed and published in an impartial manner by a wholly trustworthy source, much of it will be wasted. The promised referendum will not be a valuable complement and corrective to the failings of representative democracy, but simply another demonstration of the power of governments to manage and manipulate public opinion.

# 8

# The case for an EU research agency in the UK

From all that has been said, it will be clear that there is a strong case for the creation of a publicly-funded research agency or audit office, permanently dedicated to the analysis of the impact of EU membership on the UK economy, its costs as well as its benefits, and publishing regular reports to inform parliamentary and public debate.

A number of think tanks and pressure groups, especially eurosceptic ones, have of course already contributed a fair amount of research on regulation, immigration, trade and other subjects. However, the scale and scope of some of the relevant issues are far beyond their resources. Many of these issues require continuous funding and commitment by an agency with full-time researchers with ready access to all UK government and EU sources and informants.

Behind the trade data reported above, for instance, there are a host of issues that merit extended analysis. The data itself often deserves some scrutiny, with a reliable and trustworthy methodology for discounting the Netherlands' distortion of trade data, as well as the analogous 'Netherlands effect' that bedevils comparative analyses of FDI.[1] Comparative national data cannot take one far in trying to understand or explain temporal or cross-societal variations and none of the preceding analyses has tried to explain any of the cross-national differences identified. To do that, detailed sectoral and sub-sectoral variations, identifying industries that have lost or gained ground under the Single Market are required. Apart from enabling the CBI and other trade associations to defend their members' interests more competently, they might also determine whether the decline in the rate of growth of UK exports of goods which has accompanied the Single Market might be reasonably attributed to one or other part of that programme.

Free trade agreements present their own distinctive set of difficult problems. The missing evidence in the earlier discussion was comparative analysis and grading of the substantive provisions of the FTAs of various countries. We know that far fewer of them have included services, but it is of some importance to discover why that is so, when those of Switzerland, the US and other countries routinely include services. This would probably require interrogation of past EU trade commissioners, negotiators, intensive comparative analysis of the content of current FTAs, and access to confidential records, which an independent researcher will find more difficult than one backed by the authority of a member government. Only when we have a reasonable explanation of the failures and limitations of past agreements negotiated by the EC, will it be possible to decide whether the extension of the Single Market in services, which successive British prime ministers have urged, is a realistic aspiration or whether there are inherent and insuperable obstacles in negotiating services agreements simultaneously on behalf of 28 countries. And without some agreed and regularly published measures of the present extent of the Single Market in services, it is difficult to make much sense of the continual calls for its further extension.

It is also of interest to understand the strategy of the EC trade negotiations over past decades. It has obviously differed from that of the Swiss and other small countries, presumably for some good reason, but this has never been publicly declared or debated. Purely from a British point of view, it is of some interest to discover why FTAs with Commonwealth countries seem to have been given such a low priority by the EC, seem to take such an inordinately long time, and have such a low success rate. Even more interesting would be to discover why the TTIP negotiations which Gordon Brown referred to in 2003 (when the Swiss were already negotiating with the US) as if they were imminent, did not begin until 2013.[3] An awful lot of freer trade has been lost over those intervening years. There cannot, one need hardly add, be any sensible assessment of the strategy until we know far more about the consequences for UK exports of the agreements they have already negotiated. That requires research on a scale far beyond the resources of private interest groups sustained by voluntary subscriptions, and is evidently also far beyond the capabilities of the CBI and other trade federations that made submissions to the Foreign Office. The last CBI report on the EU, despite being over 70 pages long, relied for its estimate of the EU's trade benefits on a mishmash of older pro-EU academic papers, with no independent data or verification whatever.[4]

Another topic which few individual researchers or think tanks have either the time, or inclination to study in depth, is the reliability or trustworthiness of the public and private models that have been used to justify one or other EU policy. Optimism about, confidence in, and legitimacy of, EU policies have been largely driven by forecasts of models whose trustworthiness and reliability have rarely, if ever, been publicly tested and evaluated.[5] In the nature of things, model-building is a task in which the charlatan and the honestly-misguided can participate and thrive alongside the honest and competent. Indeed, since in EU debates an optimistic prediction is itself usually the end product of the exercise, who can ever distinguish between them? The historical track records of predictions made with these models, including the EU's own Quest model, deserves close scrutiny and comparative evaluation, particularly in regard to their predictions about the fate of individual member countries.[6]

If an agency studying these, and the many other issues that have figured in the EU debates, is to command parliamentary and public respect, it must of course be sharply distinguished from, and independent of, government departments like the BIS or the Treasury, both of which seem in past years to have been largely preoccupied with trawls for evidence on EU issues that appears to support the policy preferences of their current political masters. There are occasional exceptions to the rule, most notably the outstanding 'five tests' research on the euro, conducted by a group from within the Treasury, and perhaps the Foreign Office with regard to the balance of competences. In limited respects, both provide helpful precedents of the relationship that an independent research agency might establish with its host department. But they were exceptions to the work of these departments, both of which have otherwise been, for many years, little more than cheerleaders for EU membership.

A newly-created EU research agency has to break decisively with that tradition and mindset. It has to be akin to the National Audit Office, the Office for Budget Responsibility, or perhaps the Office for National Statistics; that is to say, it has to be an agency or department whose primary obligation is to provide trustworthy, impartial evidence to the British parliament and people, rather than providing data that current ministers want to hear. There is one body that has in recent years come closer to what is required than all those mentioned: the House of Commons Library. Its intermittent papers on the EU already display both the competence and impartiality that such an agency has to establish rather quickly, and therefore has a head start to perform a significant role in any future referendum.[7] At present, it is also engaged in a very wide range of public policy issues, and it would therefore require a dedicated, and very much enlarged, section dealing exclusively with EU issues.

There would, come to think of it, be a certain natural justice in asking the House of Commons Library to play such a role. What is primarily at stake in any future referendum is not the economic advantages and disadvantages of membership discussed in this paper, but the sovereignty of the British parliament and people. It is therefore entirely appropriate that the agency entrusted with responsibility for providing the British people with the reliable information on which they base their decision should be situated within their own parliament.

Whichever of these current precedents might be adopted to perform the role, it is clear that the agency would have to be granted a rather special status. It would have to be free to set its own agenda and priorities, though if its mission is to inform public debate about the EU, it would presumably address the issues that have figured in those debates. However, just as the OBR does not 'provide normative commentary on the particular merits of government policies', it should never declare whether UK membership of the EU is desirable or not, since once declared, it would have a house position to defend, and be diverted from its primary mission to collect, analyse and publish reliable evidence.

It must be free to recruit whatever talent it requires, and wherever it may be found, free to outsource whenever and wherever it sees fit, free to investigate anywhere within and beyond the EU, so that it can conduct appropriate comparative studies. It should also be free to collaborate with similar independent agencies, as distinct from those funded by the EC, wherever they may be, in other EU member countries, in the US and the Commonwealth. Above all, of course, it should be free to report its findings, whenever it wishes, however inconvenient they might be to the government of the day.

Such a newly-commissioned agency could generate a more informed and lively public debate than the vacuous, ill-informed observations of former prime ministers, chancellors, ministers and EU trade commissioners. It might also enable future prime ministers and ministers to negotiate rather more effectively in Brussels, and lessen their reliance on evidence provided by the EC, or by organised pressure groups found there that are not infrequently sponsored by the EC. The main beneficiaries would be the electorate as a whole and the integrity, credibility and legitimacy of any referendum in which they are asked to vote. If the government in power decides that it is best served by a re-run of the government-managed referendum of 1975 it will have rather little legitimacy, since the reluctance of past governments to collect reliable data about the impact of membership and to publish comprehensive cost-benefit analyses of it has allowed scepticism, suspicion and distrust of their EU policy to accumulate over many years. The commissioning of such an agency would be the best possible indication that the government of the day intends that the legitimacy of this referendum should be beyond reasonable doubt.

Committed partisans on both sides would also benefit. Its work would probably help to erase the legacy of deceit and misinformation which eurosceptics believe has long prejudiced a free and fair debate about the merits of the EU, a short catalogue of which is given in Appendix J. It might even begin to revive their faith in representative government which appears to have been badly shaken by the way in which successive governments have handled the EU issue. Tri-party agreement among the political elite left a significant body of opinion about the EU wholly unrepresented, until the appearance of UKIP. With data to hand from an unimpeachable source, europhiles could rely less on evidence-lite endorsements by former political luminaries with their records to defend. They would also have less need of disparaging stereotypes of those who do not share their views.[8]

Whichever way the referendum goes, such an agency could continue to play a major role in UK trade policy since the 27 other countries of the EU would remain important trading partners, and British trade intelligence is manifestly not of a particularly high standard at present. If the UK voted to remain a member, its work would be of particular benefit to the victorious EU enthusiasts, since they would then, one imagines, wish to consider how the legitimacy of the EU project might be strengthened in the future. The political leaders who engineered entry to the Common Market hoped that time, inertia, and apathy might do the trick. As they got used to it, the British people would come to accept it. Forty-two years on, that hope seems misplaced.[9] Something other than time alone is evidently required.

If the referendum is conducted in the same manner as that of 1975, it will be an uphill task, whatever the majority, but even if the referendum is conducted in a scrupulously even-handed manner, there will remain a substantial disaffected proportion of the population wholly alienated from the EU project. Presumably EU enthusiasts would hope once again that this proportion would decline over time, as the merits of the EU project become evident, but it is hard to see this happening without an impartial and trustworthy verification of those merits, which is altogether independent of those responsible for UK participation in the project, and in no conceivable way a direct beneficiary of it.

Another cherished idea of EU enthusiasts is that the British should become more European in outlook, and debate and disagree about issues from a European point of view, in the manner which they think is more common on the continent. But that hardly seems likely if Brussels remains the main source of information and analyses on Europe-wide issues. How, to pluck an example at random, could even the most devoted supporter of the EU in the UK currently know whether or not there is a case for subsidiarity with regard to any present EU directive or regulation, or to any of the present responsibilities of any EC directorates-general? The EC itself has long been *de facto* both judge and jury in deciding whether the subsidiarity principle has been correctly observed, largely because it is the only agency that has information about all member countries.[10] The European Court of Justice (ECJ), like everyone else, including the minister who provoked my inquiry, is obliged to depend on the information it cares to make available.

The only case when it has had to defend its decision before the ECJ was in May 1997, when the German government argued that its deposit guarantee scheme made EU action unnecessary in this area. The court rejected its argument on the grounds that the German scheme did not apply 'if deposits in a credit institution that has branches in other member states became unavailable'. By this decision, the court seems to have decided that the limits of legitimate EU regulatory action on any particular issue are set by the deficiencies of the least effective of the member states, which would seem to render them almost limitless. Any appellant state seeking to enforce the principle, on whatever grounds, must be aware of the analogous circumstances in all the other member states, which is itself a formidable barrier to a successful appeal.[11]

Two recent incidents suggest that subsidiarity may not be quite as inert and meaningless a principle of European government as it has long appeared to be. In 2012 the commission withdrew its attempt to impose common EU rules on workers' right to strike in the face of opposition from national governments, who used the yellow card procedure set out in the Treaty of Lisbon in 2009, and argued that this right should properly be defined by member states. In 2013, it similarly withdrew a proposal to create a European public prosecutors' office. However, in both cases, the commission appears to have been making a tactical withdrawal, perhaps with a view to reintroducing its proposals at a more opportune moment in the future, since in both cases it insisted that it had not infringed the principle of subsidiarity.

The principle has, therefore, never been tested in the ECJ since 1997. If it was to end up before the court in the future, it seems likely that the 'reasoned opinion' which national governments are required to present to support their objections to a commission proposal, will require rather more than nostalgic references to long-established national practices and preferences to make their case. They will need a substantial body of supra-national evidence of a kind that a permanent research agency might well collect, especially if its work had persuaded other member countries that they too might benefit from independent, dedicated research agencies and reduce their own dependence on Brussels.

In short, an independent UK research agency, or an enlarged and dedicated House of Commons Library research staff, could be both a practical demonstration and a powerful voice of subsidiarity; a distinctively British contribution to the institutional architecture of the EU. Instead of the EC claiming as it currently does, with some justice, that it alone can see policies and problems from a European rather than a national point of view, there would exist an independent agency in a member country, and maybe in several member countries which, in time, would be equally in command of relevant trans-European evidence on contentious issues, equally capable of transcending their own national borders, of judging issues from a European point of view and enabling their own ministers, media and public to do the same. Presumably that is what EU enthusiasts wish to see.

In sum, both sides have much to gain from the creation of such an independent agency, since both would agree that the decision of the people of Britain to stay or leave should be free of myths, of unresolved paradoxes, and should be based on the best available evidence rather than misrepresentations, deceit and dreams that have been major features of the debate thus far. The British people as a whole might then be better able to live with the result of a referendum.

# Appendices

# APPENDIX A

# BIS reply to the author's FOI request

Department for Business Innovation & Skills
18 October 2013
BIS Ref: 13/1357

Dear Mr Burrage,

Re: FOI request on the economic evidence on the benefits of the Single Market

Thank you for your email of 24 September where you requested the following information:

> 'The second paragraph of written evidence submitted by your department to the House of Lords Select Committee on the European Union on 14 October 2010, said:

> 'Economic evidence shows that the Single Market has delivered substantial economic benefits . EU countries trade twice as much with each other as they would do in the absence of the Single Market programme. Given that, according to the OECD, a 10 percentage point increase in trade exposure is associated with a 4 per cent rise in income per capita, increased trade in Europe since the early 1980s may be responsible for around 6% higher income per capita in the UK.

> 'Unfortunately, you could not include footnotes, so I write to ask if you would be kind enough to help me find the 'Economic evidence' to which you were referring. It is the evidence about 'trade twice as much...' that particularly interests me, but if you

could also give a reference to the OECD source you quote in your third sentence I would be most grateful.'

Under the Freedom of Information Act 2000 ('the Act'}, you have the right to:

- know whether we hold the information you require

- be provided with that information (subject to any exemptions under the Act which may apply)

I can confirm that the Department holds the information you have requested. However, the information is already in the public domain and is therefore exempt under Section 21 of the Act as we are not required to provide information which is already reasonably accessible to you. An overview and links to this information is provided below.

A number of studies were published on the impacts of the creation of the Single Market, and these would have been considered when this evidence was submitted to the House of Lords Select Committee – for example, the 2007 ex-post assessment published by the European Commission is commonly cited, which focusses on the benefits achieved since the formal creation of the Single Market in 1992:

- llzkovitz, Dierx, Kovacs & Sousa (2007) , Steps towards a deeper economic integration: the internal market in the 21st Century – a contribution to the Single Market Review, European Commission – DG EcFin; European Economy No. 27

    (http://ec.europa.eu/economy-finance/publications/publ ication784_en.pdf)

As part of the Balance of Competences Review announced by the Foreign Secretary in July 2012, HM government has published the first tranche of reports looking at specific areas of EU competence. This included an overarching assessment of the balance of competence between the EU and Member States on the Single Market (published 22nd July 2013).

In addition to incorporating evidence submitted by experts, non-governmental organisations, business representatives, Members of Parliament and other interested parties, the Single Market report also includes a technical appendix which provides a summary of the headline results and methodologies of some of the major (ex-ante and ex post) studies that were conducted to assess the impact of the creation of the Single Market. This includes the 2007 European Commission assessment referred to above.

The Single Market report, and all supporting evidence received, can be found at the following website:

> https://www.gov.uk/government/consultations/call-for
> evidence-on-the-governments-review-of-the-balance-of-
> competences-between-the-united-kingdom-and-the-european-
> union

The reference to the increase in intra-EU trade is based on the following study:

- Fontagne, L., T. Mayer and S. Zignago, 2005, Trade in the Triad: How Easy is the Access to Large Markets? Canadian Journal of Economics , 38(4): 1401-1430.

You also requested the full reference to the OECD source quoted:

- OECD (2003), Sources of Economic Growth in OECD countries

Finally, the following e-book, which was published last year to mark twenty years since the creation of the Single Market, may also be of interest.

- HM government/CE PR (2012), Twenty Years On: the UK and future of the Single Market

> https://www.gov.uk/government/publications/twenty-
> years-on-the-uk-and-the-future-of-thesingle-market

This set of analytical papers draws together evidence about the impact the Single Market has had to date and sets out the UK government's views on where the priorities should be going forward. These include opening up services markets, progress on the digital Single Market, liberalisation of key infrastructure networks, and a better regulatory environment.

[Appeals procedure details]
  Yours sincerely,

**Elizabeth Anastasi**
Economic Adviser –
EU Economics & Single Market European Reform Directorate,
BIS

# APPENDIX B

# A 2007 report by EC staff on the impact of the Internal Market

Here follows a summary of the major conclusions of Part 3 of the January 2007 report, 'Steps towards a deeper economic integration: the Internal Market in the 21st Century – A contribution to the Single Market Review', by Fabienne Ilzkovitz, Adriaan Dierx, Viktoria Kovacs and Nuno Sousa, of the Directorate-General for Economic and Financial Affairs.[1]

Part 3 of the report is entitled 'Empirical Evidence on the Effects of the Internal Market'. As far as possible, this summary is in the authors' own words.

## Trade flows

'After an increase in the late 1990s, fuelled by trade growth with Central and Eastern Europe prior to their accession, intra-EU trade flows of goods seems to have lost momentum since 2000, particularly among the EU15... This slowdown coincided with the introduction of the single currency, which suggests that the trade boosting effect of the single currency... [has] been far less pronounced the trade effect of enlargement.'[2]

'Extra-EU exporters have, however, benefited from the suppression of intra EU trade barriers and from the application of the principle of mutual recognition. In manufacturing since 1988 and until 2003 (latest available data) the share of extra-EU suppliers... has gradually increased at the expense of domestic production.'[3]

This 'slowdown of intra-EU trade growth relative to trade growth with third partners is unsurprising given the already very intense trade flows within the EU15 and the large untapped opportunities for trade gains with third partners.' However, comparison with the US 'shows there is plenty of scope for further trade integration within the EU', especially in services. While 'services are less tradable by nature, there is little difference between trade between EU25 Member States and trade between the EU and third countries. This clearly contrasts with manufacturing where intra EU trade clearly dominates.'

As 'the internal market increases competition pressures within the EU and improves the business environment, it should also help EU firms to expand their activities beyond EU borders'. However, 'the empirical evidence shows EU firms less active in fast-growing markets, and they have not improved their performance at world level, although this was one of the main goals of the 1992 Single Market programme. In the mid-1980s, the EU was insufficiently specialised in high-tech sectors and losing market share at world level. This situation has not changed dramatically since.'[4]

A significant part of EU trade is concentrated in intermediate skills sectors whereas other high-income regions, like the US and some South-East Asian economies, are more specialised in products requiring high to high-intermediate skills. In sectors where most of the growth in world exports is realised (like semiconductors, passenger cars, telecommunications, computers, computer parts and pharmaceuticals), the EU was only able to keep its market position but not to improve it. 'The noticeable lag of the EU with respect to ICT industries can be attributed to the lack of progress so far in the creation of a competitive internal market for services (which are the main consumers of ICT) and to a European innovation deficit.'[5]

## Foreign direct investment

Overall, in the years following the implementation of the internal market programme, intra-EU FDI activity in the EU15 has increased, and the accumulated stocks of inward and outward FDI 'have expanded spectacularly'. The increasing share of intra-EU FDI flows in total EU FDI activity 'suggests that the internal market had a role to play'.[6]

'As the European internal market becomes more integrated and efficient, it is expected to become more attractive for foreign firms.'

However, 'the available evidence suggests that the internal market has not been able to deliver in terms of global investment flows. Since 2001 the volume of FDI from the rest of the world into the EU25 has gradually declined, and only recovered slightly in 2005. The internal market two-fold objective of making the EU a more attractive place for foreign investors and of boosting the presence and competitive position of EU firms in world markets seems far from being achieved.'[7]

## Mergers and acquisitions

'In the late 80s, cross-border M&A increased at a much faster rate than domestic M&A, which suggests that they were increasingly used as a channel for market access rather than as a means for domestic restructuring. The EMU [European Monetary Union] provided added incentives for M&A in the euro area, reversing the downward trend of the early 1990s, though the ratio of cross-border acquisitions by eurozone firms has declined in 2005 to the 2000 level.' The 2004 enlargement triggered an increase of M&A operations in the new member states.

The 'share of intra-EU cross-border deals in the total number of M&A in network industries (telecom, post, utilities and transport) has increased from 15-20 per cent of all M&A in the mid-1990s to over 25 per cent more recently. Despite this positive evolution, the integration of markets in these sectors remains still limited and incumbents continue to dominate domestic markets.'

M&A data show 'the same picture' as FDI in that the 'share of the EU in the number of targeted firms in M&A operations has continuously decreased since the 1990s. 'The evidence regarding EU firms as bidders in foreign markets also suggests subdued dynamism' relative to firms from the rest of the world, particularly in the fast growing Asian service sectors.[8]

## Price dispersion and price levels

'The increased market integration has accelerated price convergence among EU15 member states, and especially in the EU25 as the new member states progressively adopt the internal market *acquis*.

However 'this process, particularly within the EU15, has slowed down in recent years' and the EMU does not seem to have added much dynamism to price convergence. Within it, price convergence is close to being exhausted, even though 'price dispersion in services remains relatively high', and 'prices in network industries still vary greatly across member states, reflecting to some extent their different degree of market deregulation.'

In the high-income member states, price levels have converged downwards towards the EU25 average, while 'in the new and lower income EU15 Member States price levels have converged upwards towards the EU25 average'. The UK is in the middle of the lower income member states in this respect, having had high price increases over the period, but this was because its 'prices at the start of the period were among the lowest of the higher income member states.'[9]

## Competition

Despite the recent slowdown in market integration and price convergence, 'the internal market and the EMU have facilitated market entry by new firms and reduced the ability of European firms to segment national markets geographically. There has therefore been greater instability in market leadership, especially between 1987 and 2000, by which year the leading top five companies had lost more than half of their production share to other firms and in many sectors a new market leader had emerged. There were reductions in mark-ups, particularly in the sectors most affected by the Single Market programme', but 'EU product markets remain heavily regulated, business dynamism is insufficient and price rigidities are persistent, with particularly high price stickiness in services.'

Firms in the internal market have expanded in size and increased their presence beyond national borders. Whereas in 1987 EU leading firms were on average active in three countries, this number increased by 2000 to an average of five countries. Simultaneously EU firms concentrated their activities in their core business. The number of sectors in which leading firms were active declined from an average of 4.9 in 1987 to 3.3 in 2000.

## Business dynamism

Rules and regulations in Europe appear to act as a constraint on the mobility of economic activity to more productive sectors and regions. In most EU countries it is still more difficult to start a new business than in the US, and the US-EU 'gap in exit rates is even wider'. Moreover, new businesses in the US 'grow much faster and reach higher average sizes in terms of employment.'

## Innovation

'The internal market does not seem to have been a sufficient catalyst for innovation and resource reallocation towards technology intensive activities. The EU innovation environment remains weak in a number of key "input" indicators, such as the amount of public and private R&D [research and development] and the stock of science and technology researchers, as well as weaknesses in the higher education system. The internal market is also losing its attractiveness for international R&D investment. Multinational companies prefer to carry out their R&D activities in the US – and more recently in China and India - rather than in the EU.'

## Conclusion: the macro-economic impact

'The internal market is essentially a series of microeconomic reforms which together have a potentially significant macroeconomic impact. It is not straightforward however to derive the aggregate impact of a series of reforms which are spread out over time and affect sectors with quite different characteristics.' To identify this impact we adopted 'three strands of analysis. First, macroeconomic impact of EU-15 market integration in manufacturing is estimated by simulating the competition and innovation effects... Second, a more targeted simulation of the macroeconomic impact of the opening up to competition of the electricity and telecommunication markets... Third, the competition and innovation effects of the increased trade in the enlarged EU of 25 member states has been simulated.'[10]

'To compute the combined effect of EU15 integration and the enlargement, the corresponding yearly mark-up and total factor productivity shocks have been added up. These… show that the enlarged internal market… is an important source of growth and jobs. As a result of the progress made over the period 1992-2006 in achieving an enlarged internal market of 25 member states, GDP and employment levels have increased significantly. The estimated 'gains' from the internal market in 2006 amount to 2.2 per cent of EU GDP (or 223 billion euro) and 1.4 per cent of total employment (or 2.75 million jobs). These gains could have been substantially larger if services market had been fully opened up to cross-border competition.'[11]

# APPENDIX C

# On Scotch, bourbon and other unconvincing business arguments for UK membership of the EU

Of all the submissions to the balance of competences review, that presented by the Scotch Whisky Association was the most warmly enthusiastic about the merits of EU membership. Unlike many others, its support for the EU and the present balance of competences was unqualified, and supported by a few telling details of the specific features of EC actions that had helped the association and presumably its members. Somehow it could not be filed as convincing evidence of the case for membership, and this note seeks to explain why.

The association opened its case by saying that the 'EU internal market, in which one set of common rules applies, is immeasurably simpler than the alternative in which 28 different regulatory regimes would operate'.[12] No one would or could disagree. However, it is not clear that this is much of an argument for continued EU membership, since non-members also benefit from one common set of rules, and if the UK decided not to remain a member it is hardly likely that the other 27 would then revert to their diverse regulatory regimes, or that a newly independent UK would find it any more difficult than exporters in numerous other non-member countries to work to the EU's common set of rules.

The association's submission then went on to say:

> EU rules, agreed with considerable and very helpful input from UK officials and MEPs, impact on almost every facet of trade in Scotch Whisky. These include: spirits definitions; protection of 'geographical indications' (such as Scotch Whisky); labelling;

taxation; a standardised range of bottle sizes; holding and movement of excisable products; and environmental issues.

They then supported unspecified benefits in EU FTAs, the 'numerous trade barriers' that have been removed, and EU support in 'four WTO dispute settlement panels dealing with tax arrangements for spirit drinks in various countries'.

Scotch whisky may, one suspects, have been rather peculiarly favoured in this respect, given that whisky is not distilled in many other EU countries. However, there is no arguing with these advantages, which leads one to expect that the association will have no difficulty demonstrating the EU's impact on its members' sales in the Single Market (which competitors from non-members countries have not enjoyed), or perhaps in wider world markets as a result of EU FTAs.

No such evidence is given or cited, so one has to try to find it for oneself by examining the exports to the EU of a distilled spirit industry in a non-member country which competes with Scotch. Bourbon distilled in Kentucky and elsewhere in the southern US is as close as we can get, though that is not very close, since bourbon has only begun to be sold internationally in relatively recent decades, whereas Scotch has long been, as the association proudly puts it, 'the world's foremost internationally traded spirit drink'.

In 1993 total sales of Scotch to the other founder members of the Single Market was more than 11 times larger than the total sales of bourbon to them plus the UK ($1.2bn versus $105m), and nearly 15 times larger without the UK ($81m). However, over the years 1993 to 2014, exports of Scotch to the EU have grown erratically with a real CAGR of just 1.62 per cent. Sales of bourbon have, by contrast, grown steadily, with a real CAGR of 8.6 per cent, and without the UK its major EU market, of 8.3 per cent.[13] As a result, after 22 years enjoying the many benefits mentioned of the Single Market, the growth in exports of Scotch to the EU by 2014 was less than four times the value of the growth of bourbon, and with the UK, less than three times.

Scotch is still number one, and still by quite a margin, but nonetheless something seems to have been happening within the Single Market of which the association is unaware. EU membership and evidently harmonious relationships with the EC do not appear to have counted for much.

If the association had wished to make a convincing case for the benefits of EU membership, it might have shown that, without those benefits, the growth rate of Scotch over 22 years would have been still less than 1.62 per cent per annum, or that of bourbon would have been still higher than 8.3 or 8.6%, or both. Their case would have been even more compelling, if it had also shown that while bourbon exports had gained rather little from US trade agreements with Korea, Australia, Singapore and others, its own members have gained considerably more from what it refers to as 'the EU's expertise and the negotiating muscle in the areas of trade policy and market access globally'. Presumably, it was referring to the EU's recent agreements with Cameroon, Moldova and Georgia.

The disconcerting aspect of the Scotch Whisky Association submission is that it did not mention any consequences for the exports of their members, nor indicate the least interest in measuring the impact of the EU or its FTAs. In other words, evidence central to the case was missing, and this is far from an isolated example. Here are a couple more examples.

Sir Gerry Brimstone, the chairman of Standard Life, a major UK insurance company, is recently reported to have said that 'the Single Market is vital to the UK' and it 'would be disastrous for London and the UK if the UK were to leave the Single Market... Why on earth would we not want to be part of one of the biggest markets in the world?'[14] The missing element in this argument is that he did not explain what being 'part of' this market means. Measured by the value of their exports, many non-EU member countries are as much a 'part of' the Single Market as the UK or any other member. It is unclear, therefore, why the UK could not and still be just as much 'a part of' the Single Market, after leaving other members to continue to construct a superstate, or whatever it is that 'ever closer union' entails.

Press reports, of course, often quote selectively, but one can see the same limitations in the considered arguments of important business representatives. Some months ago, John Cridland, director-general of the CBI , in an op-ed piece for *The Times*, sought to persuade its readers that leaving the EU was a fearsome prospect for the UK, by saying: 'Switzerland still has no agreement to ensure access to the European market in services — a major part of the UK economy.' Somehow or other he forgot to tell readers of *The Times* that Switzerland's exports of services to the EU27 over the years 2004-2012 had grown, in real terms, by 54 per cent, at a CAGR of 5.5 per cent, while the UK's had grown by just 20 per cent at a CAGR of 2.3 per cent.[15] His organisation went on to publish a 180-page booklet on the merits of EU membership.[16] The headline item on the benefits of membership was that 'it is not unreasonable to infer from a literature review that the net benefit arising from EU membership is somewhere in the region of 4–5 per cent of UK GDP... roughly the economies of the North East and Northern Ireland taken together... [which] suggests that each UK citizen has benefited from EU membership to the tune of around £1,225 every year for the last 40 years'.[17]

Net presumably means net of all the costs of the EU to the UK, which have been variously estimated as between 4 per cent and 11.5 per cent of EU and/or UK GDP. This means that the gross benefit of EU membership is, by the CBI's calculation, somewhere between 8 per cent and 15 per cent of UK GDP. This is far beyond the credible, and far advanced into the absurd. A few years earlier the EC itself had estimated the internal market had contributed just 2.2 per cent to EU GDP, an estimate which ignored costs altogether, and was itself suspect on a number of grounds.[18] Moreover, the average growth of UK GDP from 1973 to 2013 was just 2.15 per cent. If it were true, as the CBI claimed, that 'the net benefit arising from EU membership is somewhere in the region of 4–5 per cent of UK GDP', the UK GDP growth, without the net benefit arising from EU membership, would have been consistently negative 'every year for the last 40 years'. Why this would have been so, the CBI does not pause to explain. Would, one wonders, member firms accept this quality of research if it involved their own products?[19]

Business seems to have it all in the EU debate, funds and human resources, the ears of ministers, the platforms, specialist PR people and media access to ensure their views are widely publicised and respectfully received. The only thing they don't have is convincing and trustworthy research to support their views.

# APPENDIX D

# The sluggish growth of GDP and of productivity in the Single Market 1993-2013

One of the aims of the Single Market was to improve the productivity of workers in member countries. In 1988 the Cecchini report, its founding document, repeatedly referred to the productivity gains that might be predicted after the creation of a Single Market.[20]

World Bank data on real GDP growth per capita in $(2005)US over the 21 years 1993-2013, shown in Figure 10, compares the 12 founder members of the Single Market with 10 independent countries, consisting of nine OECD members plus Singapore. The three of these OECD countries in Europe, Switzerland, Norway and Iceland, are also shown separately. It may be seen that real growth of the GDP per capita, or productivity, of the founder

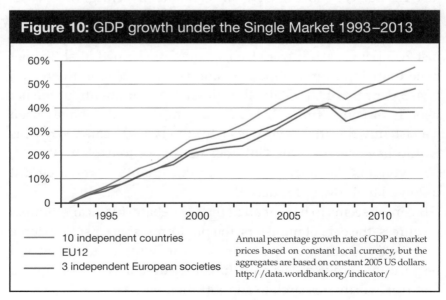

**Figure 10:** GDP growth under the Single Market 1993–2013

—— 10 independent countries

—— EU12

—— 3 independent European societies

Annual percentage growth rate of GDP at market prices based on constant local currency, but the aggregates are based on constant 2005 US dollars. http://data.worldbank.org/indicator/

members of the Single Market has been rather slower than that of other OECD members.

Table 10 gives the compound annual growth rate (CAGR) of individual countries over the period, and the weighted means of both groups. Only three member countries – Ireland, Luxembourg and the UK – have exceeded the mean growth rate of the other nine OECD countries.

**Table 10:** CAGR of GDP real growth per cap 1993-2013 in US(2005)$

| EU12 | | OECD 9 | |
|---|---|---|---|
| Belgium | 1.37 | Australia | 1.85 |
| Denmark | 1.12 | Canada | 1.59 |
| France | 1.13 | Iceland | 2.08 |
| Germany | 1.28 | Japan | 0.76 |
| Greece | 0.78 | Korea | 4.16 |
| Ireland | 3.17 | NZ | 1.78 |
| Italy | 0.39 | Norway | 1.52 |
| Luxembourg | 1.72 | Switzerland | 1.13 |
| Netherlands | 1.48 | US | 1.54 |
| Portugal | 1.07 | **Mean** | **1.57** |
| Spain | 1.31 | | |
| UK | 1.64 | | |
| **Mean** | **1.18** | | |

Source: OECD dataset GDP per capita and productivity levels. GDP per head of population, USD, constant prices,2005 PPPs, USD,2005. www.oecd.ilibrary.org/statistics

On several occasions the EC report of 2007 referred to the lagging productivity growth of member countries compared with the US. The OECD database provides an updated measure of this productivity gap, by showing in percentage terms how far the productivity of each member country falls short of, or exceeds, that of the US. This data uses the more familiar measure of productivity as output per member of the labour force, or per hour worked, rather than per capita. Table 11 shows how the gap has narrowed or widened over the 21 years 1993 to 2013.

**Table 11:** Are the members of the Single Market closing the productivity gap with the US?

% gap in GDP per hour worked with respect to the USA

|  | 1993 | 2013 | % change |
|---|---|---|---|
| Belgium | 11.7 | -1.6 | -13.3 |
| Denmark | -8.5 | -5.7 | +2.8 |
| France | -6.5 | -6.9 | -0.4 |
| Germany | -5.7 | -6.9 | -1.2 |
| Greece | -45.8 | -46.3 | -0.5 |
| Ireland | -30.1 | -6.8 | +23.3 |
| Italy | -13.2 | -24.3 | -11.1 |
| Luxembourg | 41.3 | 41.9 | +0.6 |
| Netherlands | -2.1 | -5.0 | -2.9 |
| Portugal | -52.6 | -47.4 | +5.2 |
| Spain | -21.4 | -23.4 | -2.0 |
| UK | -19.8 | -25.8 | -6.0 |

Source: OECD Dataset: GDP per capita and productivity levels, Gap in GDP per hour worked with respect to the USA 1993, 2013, www.oecd.ilibrary.org/statistics

One member country, Luxembourg, had no productivity gap with the US in 1993, though in comparisons of industrial productivity, as in other respects, it bears more resemblance to an offshore financial centre (OFC) than to a normal industrial economy. Three other member countries have seen the gap narrow: Ireland most strikingly, Portugal by over five percentage points, and Denmark by nearly three points. The other eight member countries, which include the larger EU economies, have all fallen back in terms of productivity versus the US, most by rather small amounts, though Belgium by more than 13 points, Italy by more than 11, and the UK, the third largest decline, by six.

None of this evidence suggests that the Single Market programme has had a distinctive and positive impact on productivity which was shared by its members. There appears to be no EC analysis explaining why the EU fell short of the Cecchini predictions. The 2007 staff report did not do so. Having identified the failure, it merely recommended that 'more Europe' might help the EU to catch up. The World Bank and OECD data does not suggest that the 'more Europe' of the past few years has had much effect.

Overall, the wide variations among member countries suggest that the determinants of productivity growth may have rather little to do with Europe or the Single Market, and that they are peculiar to the economic, political and cultural circumstances of each nation. Members' results are no less varied than those of non-member countries. Among non-members, decisive gains were registered by Norway (+27) Korea (+17.8) and Chile (+15.2). Others, such as Switzerland (+1.4) and Australia (0) remained much the same, while New Zealand (-2.9) and Canada (-8.9) both declined.

A further hope and prediction of the founders of the Single Market was that as member countries became more integrated they would also become more alike, partly as a result of normal competitive pressures and partly because they would learn from their fellow members and adopt the best practice found amongst them. This idea recurs frequently in the Maastricht Treaty.[21] Price compression is often taken as a measure of economic integration and as an indication that competitive pressures were working as predicted.

If the variance in these measures of productivity is used for the same purpose, they give little support to the idea that member countries have become more integrated, or that their productivity has converged. In the first measure, of the growth of GDP per capita, in US(2005)$ the standard deviation was 7,910 in 1993, whereas in 2013 it had risen to 11,964.

By the second measure, the percentage distance from the US productivity, there was a marginal convergence among member countries. In 1993 the mean gap with US productivity was -12.7 per cent, and by 2013 had increased to -13.2 per cent, but the standard deviation of the percentage differences from the US was 24.9 per cent in 1993, and 23.5 per cent in 2013.

# APPENDIX E

# The FTA histories of the EU, Korea, Chile, Singapore and Switzerland

| EU | |
|---|---|
| Goods only | |
| **RTA Partner** | **Date into force** |
| EU – Overseas Countries and Territories (10) | 01-01-71 |
| Switzerland – | |
| Liechtenstein | 01-01-73 |
| Iceland | 01-04-73 |
| Norway | 01-07-73 |
| Syria | 01-07-77 |
| Andorra | 01-07-91 |
| European Economic Area (EEA) | 01-01-94 |
| Turkey | 01-01-96 |
| Faroe Islands | 01-01-97 |
| Palestinian Authority | 01-07-97 |
| Tunisia | 01-03-98 |
| South Africa | 01-01-00 |
| Morocco | 01-03-00 |
| Israel | 01-06-00 |
| Mexico | 01-07-00(G) |
| | 01-10-00(S) |
| FYR Macedonia | 01-06-01(G) |
| | 01-04-04(S) |
| San Marino | 01-04-02 |
| Jordan | 01-05-02 |
| Chile | 01-02-03(G) |
| | 01-03 05(S) |
| Lebanon | 01-03-03 |
| Egypt | 01-06-04 |
| Algeria | 01-09-05 |
| Albania | 01-12-06(G) |
| | 01-04-09(S) |
| Bosnia and Herzegovina | 01-07-08 |
| Montenegro | 01-01-08(G) |
| | 01-05-10(S) |
| CARIFORUM States EPA | 01-11-08 |
| Côte d'Ivoire | 01-01-09 |
| Papua New Guinea / Fiji | 20-12-09 |
| Serbia | 01-02-10(G) |
| | 01-09-13(S) |
| Korea, Republic of | 01-07-11 |
| E & S Africa States Interim EPA | 14-05-12 |
| Ukraine | 01-03-13 |
| Colombia and Peru | 01-08-13 |
| Central America | 04-08-14 |
| Cameroon | 01-09-14 |
| Rep. of Moldova | 01-09-14 |
| Georgia | |

| Chile | |
|---|---|
| **RTA Partner** | **Date into force** |
| Protocol on Trade Negotiations (PTN) | 11-02-73 |
| Latin American Integration Association (LAIA) (GSTP) | 18-03-81 |
| | 19-04-89 |
| Canada | 05-07-97 |
| Mexico | 01-08-99 |
| Costa Rica (C Am) | 15-02-02 |
| El Salvador (C Am) | 01-06-02 |
| EU | 01-02-03(G) |
| | 01-03-05(S) |
| US | 01-01-04 |
| Korea, Republic of | 01-04-04 |
| EFTA | 01-Dec-04 |
| Trans Pacific Strategic Economic Partnership | 28-05-06 |
| China | 01-10-06(G) |
| | 01-08-10(S) |
| India | 17-08-07 |
| Japan | 03-09-07 |
| Panama | 07-03-08 |
| Honduras (C Am) | 19-07-08 |
| Peru | 01-03-09 |
| Australia | 06-03-09 |
| Colombia | 08-05-09 |
| Guatemala (C Am) | 23-03-10 |
| Turkey | 01-03-11 |
| Malaysia | 25-02-12 |
| Nicaragua (C Am) | 19-10-12 |
| Hong Kong, China | 09-10-14 |

## Korea

| RTA Partner | Date into force |
|---|---|
| Protocol on Trade Negotiations (PTN) (APTA) | 11-02-73 17-06-76 |
| (GSTP) | 19-04-89 |
| (APTA)– Acc'n of China | 01-01-02 |
| Chile | 01-04-04 |
| Singapore | 02-03-06 |
| EFTA | 01-09-06 |
| ASEAN | 01-01-10(G) 01 05-09(S) |
| India | 01-01-10 |
| EU | 01-07-11 |
| Peru | 01-08-11 |
| US | 15-03-12 |
| Turkey | 01-05-13 |
| Australia | 12-12-14 |
| Canada | 01-01-15 |

## Singapore

| RTA Partner | Date into force |
|---|---|
| (GSTP) | 19-04-89 |
| ASEAN Free Trade Area (AFTA) | 28-01-92 |
| New Zealand | 01-01-01 |
| Japan | 30-11-02 |
| EFTA | 01-01-03 |
| Australia | 28-07-03 |
| US | 01-01-04 |
| ASEAN - China | 01-01-05(G) 01-07-07(S) |
| India | 01-08-05 |
| Jordan | 22-08-05 |
| Korea | 02-03-06 |
| Trans Pacific Strategic Economic Partnership | 28-05-06 |
| Panama | 24-07-06 |
| ASEAN - Japan | 01-12-08 |
| China | 01-01-09 |
| ASEAN - Korea | 01-01-10(G) |
| Peru | 01-05-09(S) |
| ASEAN - India | 01-08-09 |
| ASEAN – | 01-01-10 |
| Australia - New Zealand | 01-01-10 |
| Costa Rica | 01-07-13 |
| Chinese Taipei | 19-04-14 |

This table was compiled from the Regional Trade Agreement –Information System (RTA-IS) database of the World Trade Organization in January 2015.

## Switzerland

| RTA Partner | Date into force |
|---|---|
| (EFTA) | 03-05-60(G) 01-06-02(S) |
| EFTA Accession of Iceland | 01-03-70 |
| EU    Liechtenstein | 01-01-73 |
| Turkey | 01-04-92 |
| Faroe Islands * | 01-03-95 |
| Israel | 01-01-93 |
| Morocco | 01-12-99 |
| Palestinian Authority | 01-07-99 |
| Mexico | 01-07-01 |
| FYR Macedonia | 01-05-02 |
| Jordan | 01-09-02 |
| Singapore | 01-01-03 |
| Chile | 01-12-04 |
| Tunisia | 01-06-05 |
| Korea, Republic of | 01-09-06 |
| Lebanon | 01-01-07 |
| Egypt | 01-08-07 |
| SACU | 01-05-08 |
| Canada | 01-07-09 |
| Japan* | 01-09-09 |
| Serbia | 01-10-10 |
| Albania | 01-11-10 |
| Peru | 01-07-11 |
| Colombia | 01-07-11 |
| Ukraine | 01-06-12 |
| Montenegro | 01-09-12 |
| Hong Kong, China | 01-10-12 |
| China* | 01-07-14 |
| Central Am (Costa Rica and Panama) | 19-08-14 |
| Bosnia and Herzegovina | 01-01-15 |

*:not EFTA

# APPENDIX F

## A second preliminary scorecard of the effectiveness of the trade agreements of five countries

None of the businesses and trade federations that warmly commended the UK's surrender of the right to negotiate its own trade agreements have ever conducted a study to determine the impact on UK trade of the agreements negotiated by the EC on behalf of all members. Nor has the UK government. The EC began to conduct *post facto* impact studies in 2012, but neither of the two studies completed thus far isolated the impact on UK trade.[22] We may therefore safely conclude that, after 42 years of entrusting trade negotiations to the EC, no one in the UK has the least idea of whether they have helped UK exports or not.

This has not prevented Tony Blair, the CBI and a number of political and business leaders confidently assuring us of the great advantages for UK industry of the trade agreements negotiated by the EC. This appendix examines the evidence in the UN Comtrade database about UK exports before and after these EC agreements came into force to decide whether the strong and confident opinions of UK political and business leaders should, in the absence of any evidence whatsoever, be taken seriously.

In an earlier study the OECD database was used to compare UK exports of goods before and after 15 EC agreements came into force with 14 agreements Switzerland had negotiated on behalf of its exporters.[23] The study included as many years before and after the agreement came into force as possible, on the grounds that the revised terms of trade in such agreements are usually phased in over several years, and many years may pass before the full impact of any agreement is felt. In every case, an equal number of before and after years were compared, both in terms of percentage real growth in the total value of their exports to each country with which the agreement had been concluded over each period, and the real CAGR of exports during the years before and after. Agreements that had been in force for less than five years were excluded on the grounds that the CAGR for lesser periods may vary wildly, and is often unacceptably misleading. It is entirely possible, for instance, to make the EC with Korea look like a roaring success or a dismal failure merely by changing the period from three to four years.

No attempt was made in this study to identify the contemporaneous impact of other factors that might affect the exports of the two countries in the years examined. And it focused exclusively on exports to the partner country, even though the EC agreements, in addition to increasing trade, often have social and environmental goals such as improving labour conditions or gender relations in the partner country, and helping to combat climate change. The study was also limited by the data available, the most important of which was taking imports to the partner country from the UK or Switzerland, rather than their own reported exports to that country, since data on the latter were more limited than the former. It was therefore a simple, preliminary comparative measure of the effectiveness of trade agreements, provoked by strongly held and frequently expressed opinions that the EC had negotiated agreements that were superior to those that could be negotiated by an independent country, like Switzerland – or the UK.

The evidence offered little *prima facie* support for these opinions. It showed that the rate of growth of UK exports to the partner country increased after only five of the EC negotiated agreements, and in the other 10 it declined. By contrast, the rate of growth of Swiss exports to the partner country increased after nine of their agreements and declined in the other five. Moreover, the amount of growth in the nine positive Swiss cases was substantially larger than in the five UK instances of increased growth. The rate of growth more than doubled in seven of them, whereas the UK exports managed that after only two of the EC agreements, both of which were rather small markets, Syria and Lebanon.

The data presented below replicates this earlier study using an alternative source, the UN Comtrade database, and extends it, by comparing three more independent countries alongside Switzerland and the UK. It also allows us to use reported exports to partner countries rather than imports by them, and to continue the comparison for two more years – up to 2014. The countries omitted, owing to the lack of data, are slightly different.

The rules, however, remain the same: as many partner countries as possible, over as many years as possible, but always an equal number before and after, and only countries with at least five post-agreement years of trade are included. Simply for reasons of space, the CAGR is the sole measure of growth used on this occasion. The omitted countries are also listed in each case, though in the main they are omitted because these fail the minimum five years rule, but in some cases it is because there is no data for earlier years. The unshaded cells indicate CAGR greater in the post-FTA years than pre-FTA years.

The results are consistent with the earlier study in that a far higher proportion of Swiss trade agreements have been followed by an increase in the rate of real growth of exports than those negotiated by the EC on behalf of the UK. Eleven Swiss agreements out of 15 were successful by this measure, whereas only five of the 15 EC agreements were followed by an increase in UK exports. However, in the first report, the Swiss post-agreement export growth gains were visibly larger than those of the UK, but with this UN Comtrade data, this contrast disappears. Although Switzerland has far more post-agreement gains, the unweighted mean gain of the 11 Swiss agreements followed by an increase in growth was 8.9 per cent, whereas the unweighted average of the gain in UK exports, after the five EC agreements that were followed by an increase in UK exports, was nine per cent.

This apparent improvement in post-agreement mean performance of UK exports is due to the inclusion of Papua New Guinea, which was not included in the earlier study, and in the quite striking discrepancy of Chile which was reported as not having any post-agreement increase at all in the earlier study based on imports from the UK in the OECD database. This discrepancy appears to have been due to the reliance on import figures, in US1960$, which in the tenth post-agreement year, 2012, were exceptionally low.

On the basis of these preferable Comtrade export figures, Chile emerges as the partner country that has registered the highest post-agreement growth of UK exports. One other country, Israel, also changes places from a post-agreement gain of 1 per cent in the import-based comparison, to a 7 per cent fall in the present one. On the Swiss side, Israel becomes a marginal gain, having been a marginal decline, and Korea and Egypt are more significant gains.

Overall, however, the picture that emerges from the two sources of data remains the same: most Swiss agreements are followed by an increase in export growth, and most EC agreements are followed by a decline in UK export growth.

The inclusion of three small independent countries, Chile, Korea and Singapore, is interesting on two counts. First, they show Switzerland is not unique. Both Korea and Singapore also have comparable levels of increased growth following their agreements. Most of the trade agreements of all three countries have been followed by substantial increases in the rate of growth of their exports.

Second, the UK is not unique. Even more of Chile's trade agreements have been followed by a decline in the rate of growth of their exports to the new partner country. However, it should be noted that many of the declines in the post-agreement rate of growth in Chilean exports follow quite remarkable and surely unsustainable, rates of growth in exports over the pre-agreement years, such as the CAGR of 27.47 per cent of their exports to Mexico, 32.69 per cent to China, 41.6 per cent to India, and 28.34 per cent to Australia. It seems likely that many of these growth rates were destined to fall, whatever the merits of the trade agreement may have been. One can hardly say the same of the falling growth in UK exports following the EC agreements.

Obviously, since we have only reported raw data, and said nothing of the other factors that might affect trade in these

**Table 12:** Free trade agreements in five countries

**CHILE**

| Partner country | Into force | Years pre and post | Growth pre | Growth post |
|---|---|---|---|---|
| Canada | 97 | 7 | 12.96 | **31.76** |
| Mexico | 99 | 9 | **27.47** | 14.75 |
| Costa Rica | 02 | 12 | 8.43 | **10.81** |
| El Salvador | 02 | 12 | **20.17** | 6.17 |
| **EU** | **03** | | | |
| US | 04 | 11 | **6.93** | 4.01 |
| Korea | 04 | 11 | 7.23 | **7.37** |
| Switzerland | 04 | 11 | 15.86 | **16.92** |
| Norway | 04 | 11 | **4.56** | 1.74 |
| China | 06 | 9 | **32.69** | 14.95 |
| India | 07 | 8 | **41.60** | 9.03 |
| Japan | 07 | 8 | **12.98** | -1.60 |
| Panama | 08 | 7 | **29.40** | -9.34 |
| Honduras | 08 | 7 | **9.26** | -0.05 |
| Peru | 09 | 6 | **17.32** | 3.61 |
| Australia | 09 | 6 | **28.34** | 4.38 |
| Columbia | 09 | 6 | **16.46** | 8.18 |
| Guatemala | 10 | 5 | -2.84 | **10.46** |

Omitted: EU 2003; Turkey 2011; Malaysia 2012; Nicaragua 2012; Hong Kong 2014.

**KOREA**

| Partner country | Into force | Years pre and post | Growth pre | Growth post |
|---|---|---|---|---|
| Chile | 04 | 11 | 0.22 | **12.05** |
| Singapore | 06 | 9 | 7.65 | **10.49** |
| Norway | 06 | 9 | -7.79 | **6.46** |
| Switzerland | 06 | 9 | 5.74 | **7.93** |
| India | 10 | 5 | **10.80** | -2.68 |

Omitted: EU 2011; Peru 2011; U.S 2012; Turkey 2013; Australia 2014; Canada 2015.

**SINGAPORE**

| Partner country | Into force | Years pre and post | Growth pre | Growth post |
|---|---|---|---|---|
| NZ | 01 | 11 | 5.97 | **15.30** |
| Japan | 02 | 12 | 3.70 | **3.80** |
| Norway | 03 | 11 | 2.84 | **20.72** |
| Switzerland | 03 | 11 | 2.45 | **9.33** |
| Australia | 03 | 11 | 5.69 | **10.16** |
| US | 04 | 10 | **-1.03** | -2.13 |
| India | 05 | 9 | **6.62** | 5.88 |
| Jordan | 05 | 9 | 10.32 | **20.06** |
| Korea | 06 | 8 | **14.75** | 7.21 |
| Panama | 06 | 8 | 17.10 | **20.04** |
| China | 09 | 5 | **15.42** | 13.78 |
| Peru | 09 | 5 | 16.60 | **31.75** |

Omitted: Costa Rica 2013; Taipei 2014.

## Table 12: Free trade agreements in five countries *continued*

**SWITZERLAND**

| Partner country | Into force | Years pre and post | Growth pre | Growth post |
|---|---|---|---|---|
| Turkey | 92 | 4 | -2.78 | **16.87** |
| Israel | 93 | 6 | -4.45 | **1.09** |
| Morocco | 99 | 11 | -2.20 | **9.40** |
| Mexico | 01 | 13 | 5.03 | **7.39** |
| Jordan | 02 | 13 | 5.34 | **10.48** |
| Singapore | 03 | 12 | 2.65 | **9.65** |
| Chile | 04 | 11 | -2.93 | **7.32** |
| Tunisia | 05 | 10 | 1.06 | **12.50** |
| Korea | 06 | 9 | 0.63 | **8.03** |
| Lebanon | 07 | 8 | **7.1** | 6.7 |
| Egypt | 07 | 8 | -0.03 | **10.63** |
| Canada | 09 | 6 | **13.45** | 7.27 |
| Japan* | 09 | 5 | **6.07** | 0.34 |
| Serbia | 10 | 5 | -3.19 | **2.35** |
| Albania | 10 | 5 | **12.72** | -2.68 |

Omitted: Faroe Islands 1995; Palestinian Authority 1999; FYR Macedonia 2002; SACU 2008; Peru, Colombia 2011; Ukraine, Montenegro, Hong Kong 2012; China, Costa Rica, Panama 2014.

**UK**

| Partner country | Into force | Years pre and post | Growth pre | Growth post |
|---|---|---|---|---|
| Turkey | 96 | 3 | 8.06 | **8.36** |
| Tunisia | 98 | 5 | **15.81** | 2.25 |
| Morocco | 00 | 7 | **14.16** | -4.13 |
| Israel | 00 | 7 | **9.29** | 2.24 |
| Mexico | 00 | 7 | **5.56** | -2.27 |
| Jordan | 02 | 9 | **0.73** | 0.63 |
| Chile | 03 | 10 | -2.30 | **17.06** |
| Lebanon | 03 | 10 | 0.19 | **5.05** |
| Egypt | 04 | 11 | **2.46** | 1.18 |
| Algeria | 05 | 10 | **11.52** | 10.56 |
| Albania | 06 | 9 | **4.88** | -1.27 |
| Bosnia & Herz | 08 | 7 | **7.26** | -1.70 |
| Côte d'Ivoire | 09 | 6 | **8.83** | 6.69 |
| Papua N Gn | 09 | 6 | -15.36 | **1.11** |
| Fiji | 09 | 6 | 4.47 | **8.53** |

Omitted : Members' Overseas Countries & Territories (10), Switzerland – Liechtenstein, Iceland, Norway, 1971; Syria 1977; Andorra 1991; Faroe Islands & Palestinian Authority 1997; South Africa 2000; FYR Macedonia 2001; San Marino2002; Montenegro & CARIFORUM States 2008; Serbia 2010; Korea 2011; E & S Africa States 2012; Colombia and Peru & Central America Customs Union 2013;Cameroon & Moldova & Georgia 2014

Source: United Nations Commodity Trade Statistics Database (COMTRADE) www.comtrade.un.org

countries before and after the trade agreements considered, we can only conclude that there is strong *prima facie* evidence that, if the goal of an FTA is to increase exports to a partner country, Korea, Singapore and Switzerland have usually negotiated effective trade agreements, whereas most of those negotiated by the EC, and Chile, have been ineffective.

The main value of this data therefore is to raise questions. In the case of the political and business leaders in the UK who have for many years been singing the praises of letting the EC negotiate its trade agreements on Britain's behalf over the past 42 years, on the grounds of its 'heft' and 'clout', these are very serious questions.

Table 13 lists some of the differences between the five countries considered above.

| | No of agreements examined | Pre-agree-ment mean CAGR % | Post-agree-ment mean CAGR % | No of gains | No of falls | Gain/ fall ratio |
|---|---|---|---|---|---|---|
| **Table 13:** An FTA effectiveness scorecard | | | | | | |
| Chile | 17 | 16.0 | 7.4 | 5 | 12 | -0.4 |
| Korea | 5 | 3.3 | 6.8 | 4 | 1 | 4 |
| Singapore | 12 | 8.3 | 13 | 8 | 4 | 2 |
| Switzerland | 15 | 2.6 | 7.2 | 11 | 4 | 2.75 |
| UK | 15 | 5.0 | 3.6 | 5 | 10 | -0.5 |

# APPENDIX G

# The fanciful CER model of the trade benefits of EU membership

A note on 'The economic consequences of leaving the EU: The final report of the CER commission on the UK and the EU Single Market', John Springford, Simon Tilford, Philip Whyte, Centre for European Reform, (June 2014) with particular reference to the supposed benefits of the EU membership for UK trade.

The executive summary of this final report of a Centre for European Reform (CER) 'commission' announced that the centre had constructed an economic model, which showed that Britain's EU membership 'has boosted its trade in goods with other member states by 55 per cent'. The *Financial Times* of 9 June 2014 devoted its entire page three to summarising its major points under the headline 'Benefits of leaving the EU are illusory'. Few research reports get this kind of news coverage, but then the report happened to lend support to the *FT*'s longstanding editorial stance. This note is to explain why the report, and its headline claim, is ignored in this investigation.

The claim that EU membership has boosted UK trade with other members by 55 per cent derives from an *ad hoc* model which the CER constructed for its own commission. Its rationale and methodology can be briefly described in the report's own words. After helpfully noting 'the fact that the EU remains the UK's largest trading partner might have nothing to do with Britain's EU membership', it continued:

> To capture the effect that membership of the EU has on UK trade, factors that determine the amount of trade between countries must be controlled for: economic size, distance from Britain, whether the trading partner's citizens

speak English and so on. If these factors are held constant and Britain still trades more with the EU than with countries outside the bloc, then that additional trade is attributable to membership of the EU.

The CER has constructed a 'gravity' model to measure the EU's role in creating and diverting trade between Britain, the EU and its 30 largest trading partners that are not EU members. Together, these countries account for almost 90 per cent of Britain's trade. We took data on the total value of goods traded – exports and imports – between Britain and 181 countries between 1992 and 2010. We then took data on the countries' GDP and their real exchange rates, and by using a statistical technique called fixed effects, took into account other factors that affect trade, such as countries' populations, their distance from Britain and so on. Allowing for these factors, the UK's trade with the other EU members is 55 per cent higher than one would expect, given the size of these countries' economies and other controls… In 2013, Britain's bilateral goods trade with the EU was £364 billion, so this 'EU effect' amounted to around £130 billion.[24]

While the claim that EU membership has been very good for UK trade is clear, the moment one tries to put the argument in a form that enables one to see whether it is consistent with other known facts about UK trade with the EU it is rather less so. For instance:

- No time scale is given, and nothing is therefore said about over what years this 55 per cent increase might have occurred. Since it claims that 'EU membership has boosted UK trade with other member states', one might at first glance take it to mean that this 55 per cent increase has been distributed over the entire 42 years of EU membership. However, the report also acknowledges that 'after an initial expansion in the proportion of British trade conducted with the EU in the 1980s and 1990s, it levelled off'. And they then add that 'the proportion conducted with the EU11… fell over the last decade'. They give no specifics of this levelling off, or of the recent fall, so the reader is left to wonder about the contrast between the Common and Single Market. In the end, one must assume, that the reader is supposed to ignore these variations over time, and to conclude that by 2012 UK trade with the EU11 was 55 per cent higher than it would have had the UK not become a member of the EU in 1973.

- Although the report refers to 'trade with the EU' and 'trade between Britain and other member states' and 'trade with other EU members', it never gives the actual number of member states included in the analysis. Because of the remark just quoted, we may assume that the commission is referring to the trade conducted with the EU11, and that it has taken these 11 to stand for EU members as a whole over the entire period of UK membership rather than a continuously increasing number of members.

- We may also assume that, though they refer to EU membership, they are in fact referring to the specific years from which their data is drawn, which would probably mean from 1992-2010, though in the short appendix on the model it refers to data from 1980 to 2010.[25]

The model is not integrated with any other arguments and evidence in the report, but added like a cherry to a cake. Nothing more is said about the other 181 countries about which evidence was collected, and there are no historical or comparative references, so that the finding that EU membership has boosted UK trade by 55 per cent appears out of the blue, with no findings or citations that might help to verify or corroborate it. One only hopes that there has not been a typographical error, and that it was not a 25 per cent or 75 per cent boost to UK trade. No one could be any the wiser. Whatever the figure is, the reader is expected to take it on trust.

One simple way to decide whether or not to do so, is to compare the growth of the exports of independent OECD countries, who are neither members of the EU, nor of the EEA, with the growth of UK exports over the same period, to the same 11 EU countries, minus of course the 55 per cent boost to UK exports that the model suggested is due to EU membership. We will therefore be examining what the CER model suggests UK exports to the EU11 would have been if it had not become an EU member, and not therefore benefited from a 55 per cent boost to its exports, but had instead continued to trade with the EU like other independent OECD countries.

The model did not distinguish imports and exports. Here, simply for the sake of the argument, and because this search for benefits, like most of the debate about the merits of EU membership, has been exclusively concerned with UK exports, we will assume that the CER model showed that EU membership boosted both imports and exports equally by 55 per cent.[26]

There are nine OECD countries that have complete exports data from 1973, and whose growth may be compared with that of the UK up to 2012. We will do so in 1973 US dollars, so that we are measuring real growth, on the assumption that the model did the same. Three of these countries, Korea and Turkey and Mexico, were still developing economies at the start of the period, and relatively new world exporters and therefore not sensibly compared with the UK over this period. They recorded real growth of exports to the EU11 from 1973 to 2012 of 3,729 per cent, 1,358 per cent and 729 per cent respectively. They will therefore be excluded from the comparison of exports to the EU. We are therefore left with six remaining independent OECD countries, Australia, Canada, Israel, Japan, New Zealand and the United States.

The real growth of UK exports to the 11 fellow EU members over these 40 years was 357 per cent, and their value in 2012 was, in 1973 US dollars, $4.48bn per month, ($23.5bn in current value dollars) but after removing the 55 per cent boost they received, according to CER's model, from their EU membership, their value in 2012 was $2.89bn per month, and their real growth from 1973-2012 was 195 per cent, not 357 per cent.

If therefore the UK had been trading with the EU11 over these years like the six other independent OECD countries the growth of its exports to the EU would have been comfortably exceeded by every single one of them. Australian exports grew by 528 per cent, Japanese by 361 per cent, American by 307 per cent, Canadian by 246 per cent, Israeli by 232 per cent and New Zealand's by 216 per cent. What conceivable grounds are there for thinking that this is even a remote possibility? Let us leave intermittently war-torn Israel out of the picture: we are supposed to believe, if we choose to follow the calculations of the CER model, that as a non-member of the EU, UK exports to its EU near neighbours would have grown, since 1973, less than those of New Zealand's, even though New Zealand exports were subject to progressively increasing EU tariffs on agricultural products, and its exporters were over those years turning away from the EU and finding new markets in Asia. It seems improbable, especially as the gravity equation on which the model is based emphasizes the importance of geographical propinquity.

If we confine the comparison to the shorter period 1992-2012, the CER model makes UK exports as a non-member of the EU look still more dismal, and unbelievable. In 1992 US dollars, the value of UK exports to the EU11 in 2012 would have been, without the 55 per cent boost from EU membership, $9.1bn, instead of $14.2bn, and their real growth over these 21 years outside the EU would therefore have been just over nine per cent. Those same 21 years coincide with Japan's two 'lost decades' and during them its exports to the EU11 grew less than those of any other OECD country, but they nonetheless recorded real growth of 48 per cent. This is more than five times greater than UK exports to the EU11 would have grown, according to the CER model, if the UK had not been a member of the EU. Australia's grew by 222 per cent over these 21 years, more than those of any of the other five OECD countries, meaning that they grew more than 20 times as much as those of the UK would have done if they had not been an EU member, according to the CER model. This is not credible.

One might add that UK exports to the other nine OECD countries over these same years grew by 78 per cent, which is more than eight times greater than its exports to the 11 members of the EU, if the CER model is to be believed.

Clearly, it is not to be believed. Its headline 55 per cent claim is in the same fanciful world as the minister's claim that EU countries trade twice as much with each other as they would do in the absence of the Single Market programme. It demonstrates the limitations and hazards of claims, estimates and predictions that rest on newly-constructed *ad hoc* economic models whose performance and reliability have never been independently tested and verified against known historical records.

A further reason for ignoring the CER model is that its authors see no need to refer to an earlier estimate derived from the Treasury model, and do not try to explain why their results differed so markedly from it, and why we should prefer theirs. In 2005, a Treasury team estimated that EU membership increased UK trade with EU members by a mere seven per cent, which is at least not inconsistent with known facts, unlike the CER's claim that membership had increased UK trade by nearly eight times as much. The Treasury then sought to explain why trade between EU member states as a whole was, according to their model, 'boosted by 38 per cent', and suggested that this might be due to 'the fact that the UK was more open to trade than some member states before accession, and therefore the relative impact may have been less'.[27]

Of course, the CER model has eight or nine years of more recent evidence available to it than the Treasury, but then the CER has already told us that the proportion of UK trade with the EU 'fell over the last decade', which strongly suggests that EU membership might well have increased UK trade with its members by less than 7 per cent.

The fact that the *Financial Times* chose to take the claim seriously, and that the report in which it is made is seemingly endorsed by numerous distinguished academics and businessmen, further demonstrates that when discussing EU membership or the Single Market intelligent people will suspend their normal critical faculties, and allow hopes and impressions to cloud their better judgement.

The *Financial Times* has form in this respect – that is, in featuring 'news' that appears to lend support to UK membership of the EU, and ignoring that which doesn't. One of the striking examples occurred during the euro debate in the UK. On 26 June 2000, it carried a report on a new model constructed by a professor at the University of California, Berkeley, Andrew Rose, which predicted the trade impact of the new currency, under a bold heading across three columns saying 'Britain "could triple its trade with euro-zone"'. Rose's model had already been subject to scathing criticism, about which the *FT* said not a word. Over subsequent years, Rose's predictions of a doubling or tripling of EU trade as a result of the currency union were continuously being scaled down by other researchers, and eventually, and almost apologetically, by one sympathetic scholar in an ECB report, by 'something like five to ten per cent', while non-euro countries exports to the eurozone have grown by seven per cent. On hearing of this, the *FT* seems to have decided, on 3 July 2006, that it might not have been following and reporting the full story of the trade effects of the euro in a report opening with the question: 'Has Britain been the clever one staying out of the euro?'

By this standard we might, I suppose, expect an *FT* report correcting the impression left by the publicity it has given to the equally absurd CER calculations of the EU membership's contribution to UK exports, sometime in 2021.

# APPENDIX H

## The EU's TTIP negotiating team

**Ignacio Garcia Bercero** joined the European Commission in 1987 and has thorough experience in a large number of trade-related policy areas. During the Uruguay Round of multilateral negotiations, he followed, *inter alia*, negotiations on trade safeguards, GATT articles, functioning of the GATT, as well as talks on trade and environment. In the period leading up to the launch of the WTO Doha Round, he served as coordinator of the EU WTO policy and led the negotiations on trade and competition. He was also posted in the EU Delegation to the United Nations in New York and worked in areas of WTO Dispute Settlement and Trade Barriers Regulation. More recently, between 2005 and 2011, Mr Garcia Bercero's field of responsibility included trade-related aspects of sustainable development, as well as bilateral trade relations with South and South-East Asia, Korea, EuroMed and the Middle East countries. As the Chief Negotiator, he led the negotiating process with South Korea and India. Mr Garcia Bercero holds a Law Degree from the Faculty of Law of the Universidad Complutense, Madrid and a Master of Laws Degree (with Distinction) from University College, London.[28]

**Marco Düerkop** works in the Directorate General for Trade of the European Commission in Brussels. He is currently assistant to the Deputy Director General in charge of multilateral trade policy, trade relations with Russia and Ukraine and trade defence policy. In his former positions in the Commission, he was a member of the EU's negotiating team in the current round of WTO trade negotiations and coordinator for WTO panel cases against EU trade defence measures. Before joining the Commission in 2001, he worked in the German Foreign Office in units dealing with

NATO and UN affairs and was posted at the German Embassy in Athens as head of the Consular, Legal, and Protocol Department. He studied law at the University of Bayreuth and holds an LL.M. from the College of Europe in Bruges. He also lectures at the Willy Brandt School of Public Policy at the University of Erfurt.[29]

**Martin Merlin** is French and he speaks French, English and German. He studied international affairs, economics and philosophy in Paris. He has lectured on financial services at the European College of Parma (Italy) and at the Institut d'Etudes Politiques (Paris). He started his career at the French Treasury, where he worked for two years as a Desk Officer in the International Monetary and Financial affairs unit. He joined the European Commission in 1997 to work on insurance and pension funds issues in DG internal market. Between 2000 and 2004, he was Assistant to the Director General for the internal market. From November 2004 to January 2008 he was a member of cabinet with Commissioner Charlie McCreevy. He left the cabinet to return to DG internal market where he is Head of Unit 02, responsible for financial services policy, and relations with the Council. This unit is, *inter alia*, in charge of defining and implementing the European's Commission policy in the area of financial supervision.[30]

# APPENDIX I

## Costs and benefits of EU membership on a common scale with alternative expenditures

At several points in the preceding research we have had reason to regret the failure of any British government over 40 plus years of membership to keep a running or periodic count of costs and benefits of membership of the EC or the EU.[31] When comparing the growth of UK exports with those of non-members, we could only mention that the reader should bear in mind that the UK exports have incurred costs that those of non-members have not, but no allowance was made in the comparative graphs or tables for these extra costs, and no suggestion made about how this might be done.

A second and more important reason for regret at the lack of research is that UK taxpayers and consumers must remain unaware of the contribution they have made over these 40 years to reducing the trade costs of companies that export to the EU. In effect, they have unknowingly been paying a subsidy to these companies, the size of which the successive governments have, for their own reasons, declined to measure. It is not known whether the present Conservative government thinks that voters should be any more informed about the costs and benefits of membership when they come to vote in a referendum. Thus far, they have given no indication that they wish to break with past practice, in which case voters will have to weigh the costs and benefits for themselves.

This is not an easy task, and this appendix is intended to offer modest – very modest – assistance on one of the difficulties. If they have kept track of politicians' claims about the benefits of EU membership for the UK, they will find that many of the alleged benefits are impossible to measure, which means we have to accept the speaker's word that they exist at all, while the costs are seldom mentioned at all. Even when they are expressed as a measured value, the units chosen to measure both costs and benefits vary widely. They are sometimes expressed as a percentage of total GDP growth, sometimes for the EU as a whole, sometimes per capita, or per household, sometimes in euros, sometimes in pounds sterling, or when international sources are used in US dollars, and sometimes in nominal values and sometimes in constant value of a given year. Even then, the difficulties are not quite over, since they often switch between millions or billions of euros or pounds, sums that are so far beyond everyday experience that it is easy to lose track of their real value, especially as one side in the debate treats them as astonishingly large, while the other portrays them as too trivial to get worked up about relative to the size and scale of the national economy.

The purpose of this appendix is to express some of the items that might figure in anyone's cost/benefit analysis of EU membership in a common unit of account, so that both costs and benefits are more readily intelligible. The chosen unit of account is billions of pounds sterling, and so that one is not confused by changes in the value of sterling over time, the items discussed are all chosen from a single year, 2013. This is the most recent year for which one can be sure of a full complement of relevant data in published sources.

The results are presented in Figure 11 which contains three kinds of measure: the blue columns 5 and 6 refer to the most frequently claimed benefits of EU membership, UK exports to fellow members, the black and grey columns 1 to 4 on the left hand side depict the reported and estimated costs of membership, and the multi-coloured ones on the right hand side refer to other items of public expenditure in the UK, as a yardstick by which we grasp the scale of both the benefits and costs of EU membership. Each of these deserves a word of explanation.

## A measureable benefit: exports to the EU

Enthusiasts of the EU claim there are many benefits from membership, but unfortunately these other benefits can seldom, if ever, be reliably measured. The former prime minister, Tony

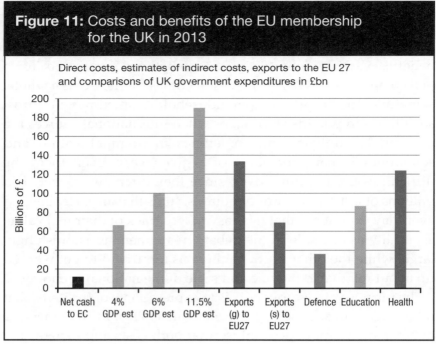

**Figure 11:** Costs and benefits of the EU membership for the UK in 2013

Direct costs, estimates of indirect costs, exports to the EU 27 and comparisons of UK government expenditures in £bn

Sources:
OECD Quarterly International Trade Statistics Dataset, Exports, Annual, UK; Trade in Services Dataset, EBOPS 2002, United Kingdom, Total Services, Exports, both in millions of US (2013) Dollars; Millions of US (2013)dollars;
UK GDP Statistical bulletin: Gross Domestic Product Preliminary Estimate, Quarter 1 (Jan to Mar) 2015, data section, Figure 2, GDP (£billion) and quarter-on-quarter growth 1, Quarter 1 (Jan to Mar) 2015, UK, 2003 to 2015,
http://www.ons.gov.uk/ons
HM Treasury , Public Expenditure Statistical Analyses 2014. p.74, Table 5.4 Public Sector current and capital expenditure on services by function 2012-2013, Cm8902, July 2014
https://www.gov.uk/government/uploads/system/uploads/attachment_data/file/330717/PESA_2014
http://ec.europa.eu/budget/financialreport/2013/lib/financial_report_2013_en.pdf
Sources of the three cost estimates are given in the text.
A measureable benefit: exports to the EU

Blair, has referred to the 'global leadership role' which he thinks EU membership allows Britain to play, but he is remarkably vague as to what that might be. Even if he could give some examples, it is debatable whether his own efforts to perform this global leadership role had much to do with the EU, and if they did, whether many British people would consider them a benefit, and if they did, whether and how they might be measured.

The former deputy prime minister, Nick Clegg, presumably had a somewhat similar benefit in mind when he claimed that EU membership enabled Britain 'to walk tall in Beijing, New Delhi and Washington'. This sounds like a benefit which he himself and other politicians might perhaps feel and enjoy, but which could only be measured with unacceptably wide margins of error. Two further benefits which Mr Clegg frequently emphasised are that EU membership enables the UK to deal more effectively with climate change and with international organised crime. Since the amount of global warming is itself subject to debate, the idea that we might measure the British contribution to the lowering of global temperatures, and then calculate how much of this British contribution is due to membership of the EU, seems far-fetched. In principle, it might be possible to demonstrate whether tracing and extraditing criminals is easier as an EU member, but neither Mr Clegg nor anyone else has sought to do so.[32] The current headline cases of transnational organised crime centring on FIFA, and of emission test rigging by Volkswagen, do not suggest that the EU is especially distinguished or advantaged in this respect.

In the absence of other named and measurable benefits, we are obliged, for the moment at least, to treat exports to the EU as the only measureable benefit of membership. However, there is no reason to think that in doing so we will end up with a narrow and distorted view of the benefits, since a number of the other claimed benefits, such as improvements in employment, income and productivity that it was once thought would flow from membership of the EU are primarily delivered via an increase in exports. Moreover, to maintain free access for UK exports to other members is by far the most frequently used argument for continued membership. Indeed for many it is not just the main reason but even the sole reason for membership. The prime minister's remark that 'our participation in the Single Market, and our ability to help set its rules, is the principal reason for our membership of the EU' would appear to place him among the former, though it is not entirely certain because he did not give any other reasons.

The two blue columns give the total value of UK exports of goods and services in 2013. Some proportion of the £202.3bn of exports to other EU members (£133.2bn of goods exports, and

£69.1bn of services) is attributable to membership of the EU, and to the benefits of the Single Market. But what proportion? It is hardly possible that all of these exports have been derived from membership of the EU since, before joining, the UK had substantial exports to the then member countries and to most of those countries that have since become members. Our next problem therefore is to determine what proportion of the £202.3bn of exports to other EU members is attributable to membership of the EU, and to the benefits of the Single Market.

## What proportion is attributable to EU membership?

In an attempt to measure what extra proportion of these exports of goods might reasonably be attributed to EU membership, the value of UK exports to 12 countries which were then, or have since, become members were measured as a proportion of UK GDP in 1973, and then compared with the value of UK exports to the same 12 countries as a proportion of UK GDP in 2013.[33] The proportion has declined from 18.7 per cent in 1973 to 16.5 per cent in 2013. Membership has thus been accompanied by a *decline* in the proportion of UK exports going to fellow members which makes it difficult to calculate the extra proportion that might be attributed to EU membership. No similar analysis can be conducted for services exports since service data do not go back that far.

This result flies in the face of the myth of the Single Market, though it is consistent with the preceding analysis of the decline in the growth of UK exports of both goods and services to fellow EU members during the Single Market decades, and with other data which showed that, as a proportion of all UK goods exports to all OECD countries, those to fellow members of the EC/EU declined over the years 1972-2012.

There are no reliable and trustworthy measures or estimates of the proportion of additional UK exports to EU countries that might be attributable to the UK's membership of the EU. We have examined one minister's claim to the House of Lords sub-committee in 2010 that 'EU countries trade twice as much with each other as they would do in the absence of the Single Market programme', and shown it to be false. Scarcely less absurd is the figure derived from the model of Centre of European Reform in 2014 'that Britain's EU membership has boosted its trade in goods with other member states by 55 per cent'. This has been examined in Appendix G and, regrettably, shown to be utterly implausible.

However, in 2005, a Treasury team estimated that EU membership increased UK trade with EU members by seven per cent, which is not inconsistent with known facts.[34] It was used in the balance of competences review in 2014, and we must therefore assume it remains the latest official estimate. Until some later and more trustworthy estimate is published, it constitutes the best estimate we have. However, this estimate was based on trade in goods alone, and hence we still lack the percentage of trade in services that might be due to EU membership. For the moment, we will have to assume that it is the same as goods and that the proportion of all UK trade attributable to EU membership was seven per cent, and that there was no difference in this respect between 2005 and our selected year of 2013.

If this Treasury calculation is to be believed, it would mean that £9.32bn of the £133.2bn of UK exports of goods to other EU members were due to membership of the EU, and £4.84bn of the £69.1bn of UK exports of services were attributable to membership of the EU, making a total benefit to UK exports of £14.2bn.

## Extra-EU exports

This might not be the end of the story, or the problem. One of the reasons originally given to the British people for joining the EU was that it would increase their low productivity. If this had happened, if there had been productivity increases in the UK economy, and these could reasonably be attributed to EU membership, then some proportion of UK exports to other countries should be added to the £14.2bn. It would, however, be rather difficult to calculate the proportion of exports to other countries attributable to the productivity increase that was itself attributable to EU membership. The evidence presented in Appendix D suggests that it is not necessary to try to do so, since there have not been any noticeable increases in UK productivity, at least during the Single Market years.[35] Indeed using the benchmark measure relative to the US, UK productivity seems to have declined over these years.

It is also possible that UK exports to other countries have benefited from the FTAs negotiated by the EC during the years of UK membership. However, the data presented in the text and in Appendix F indicates that in most cases these agreements have been followed by a decline in UK exports, and those in which it has been followed by an increase are, apart from Turkey, very small markets indeed. In any case, any attempt to add to the amount attributable to these markets should properly include an assessment of the value of the freer trade over many years to many larger markets that the UK has sacrificed by ceding to the EU responsibility for negotiating trade agreements. The likelihood is that if anyone were to attempt this tricky calculation, it would not warrant any increase in the proportion of UK exports attributable to EU membership, and would be rather more likely to require a reduction.

For the moment therefore we will make no adjustments, though of course we should remain ready to do so as and when trustworthy evidence becomes available.

## Four columns of real and estimated costs

The costs of membership are presented in the four columns on the left hand side. The black column on the far left shows the net cash transfers to the European Commission in the year 2013.[36] There can be little argument about the £11.5bn, since it is the net cash transfer to the EC in 2013, including those sums which the EC calls its 'own resources'. These consist of tariffs collected on imports to the UK (minus an administrative collection charge), and a small percentage of all VAT payments made in the UK. They are therefore paid by firms and consumers in the UK, and so must be counted as a cost to the UK. The figure of £11.5bn may not coincide with that recorded as paid by the Treasury and the Office for National Statistics, owing to variations in accounting conventions, and the periods of account.[37] It seemed appropriate in this context to prefer the EC figures and convert them to pounds at the mean exchange rate for the year 2013.

This £11.5bn is, of course, only the direct fiscal cost of membership to the UK, but once we try to include indirect costs, such as the costs of the CAP, the CFP, the environmental and renewable agenda, regulations and the remaining tariffs on imports, we have to rely on estimates, which inevitably provoke arguments. Since this is not the place to get involved in them, the histogram presents three estimates in the grey columns, allowing the reader to decide which they find more persuasive.

The first is that given by EC officials. Lord Mandelson was once one of them. In 2004, speaking as EU trade commissioner-designate to the Confederation of British Industry, according to the report in the *Financial Times*:

> The commissioner designate said the cost of EU red tape is roughly double the economic benefits generated by the Single Market. Regulation amounted to about four per cent of the EU's gross domestic product.

This was an unusual admission that the costs of the EU then outweighed its benefits.[38] Lord Mandelson has never confirmed or repeated it, or indeed said anything further on the subject. However, this may not matter too much since, as Civitas research fellow Jonathan Lindsell has noted, in the same year the Dutch finance minister gave exactly the same four per cent figure for the burden to the Netherlands, which suggests that the figure came from official sources within the EC. This is therefore presented as one estimate of the costs of the EU to the UK, though it obliges us to assume that what was then true of the EU as a whole, and for the Netherlands, was also true of the UK, and that there have been no significant increases or decreases between 2004 and 2013.[39] However, it is clear that the four per cent must be considered a rock bottom figure of the total costs since it does not include the direct fiscal costs, the costs of the CAP, CFP and all the other indirect costs. It was only, as Lord Mandelson put it, 'the cost of EU red tape.'

Unfortunately, the EC does not regularly publish figures of the costs of membership either for the EU as a whole or for member states, nor does it ever describe the methodology of its estimates.

Its figures come to us out of the blue. In 2006 Günther Verheugen, European Commissioner for Industry & Enterprise, stated that the average cost for member states was 5.5 per cent of GDP, though in the following year, he revised the figure down to 3.5 per cent, without giving any explanation of either figure.

Another later, out-of-the-blue EC estimate was limited to 'administrative costs'. These costs were mentioned on the EC's Better Regulation website in 2012, though only incidentally in a statement that was devoted to reducing these administrative costs. As may be seen in the screen capture, the EC website reported: 'According to estimates it would be feasible to reduce administrative costs by as much as 25 per cent by 2012. This would have a significant economic impact on the EU economy – an increase in the level of GDP of about 1.5 per cent or around €150 billion.'[40] If 25 per cent of the administrative costs amount to €150bn and about 1.5 per cent of GDP, then it seems reasonable to infer that the EU's total administrative costs were €600bn per annum and about six per cent of the EU's GDP. Obviously, it would be preferable to have a direct statement of the total administrative costs, along with an explanation of how they were collected, but in their absence, we have taken this as a second estimate, and again assumed that what was true of the EU as a whole was also true of the UK.

The third estimate by Tim Congdon is the only one that explains its methodology in some detail, that identifies and explains line by line the costs included, that focuses specifically on the UK, and that endeavours to measure all the costs, not just the costs of regulation.[41] His work is based on earlier work by Gerard Batten and has been revised annually some seven times, and attempts to draw on all the available published research over the preceding year. Congdon concluded that, in 2013, EU membership cost the UK about £185bn or 11.5 per cent of its GDP. Since the author has been an active and leading member of UKIP, it may be worth adding that he is also a distinguished economist, and that his method during this research was, as he put it, 'to avoid giving my own opinion, but to use other people's expertise and to cite other sources. With some exceptions (which I made clear in the text), every number was not mine, but that of another authority or individual.'

The multi-coloured items on the right hand side are simply a selection of items of the current and capital expenditure on various public services for 2013 taken from the Treasury's Public Expenditure Statistical Analyses (PESA). They are included in the hope that they may make it a little easier to grasp the scale of both the costs and benefits of the EU, and in much the same spirit as journalists commonly try to help us grasp the dimensions of unfamiliar objects in terms of more familiar ones, as so many football pitches, or London buses, or Eiffel Towers, and so forth.

## The final balance sheet

Having explained how the figures in the chart have been derived, we may now return to it and try to decide whether the benefits of membership are an adequate or satisfactory return for the costs of membership.

For those who think the benefits of membership are to be measured only in terms of UK exports, and that the Treasury probably made a reasonable estimate of the proportion of UK exports attributable to EU membership, (a group that probably includes the present prime minister) the calculation is fairly simple. To obtain an additional £14.2bn of UK exports of goods and services in 2013, the UK taxpayer paid the EC £11.2bn, plus whatever of the estimated indirect costs those making the assessment find most plausible: another £66.2bn if we accept Lord Mandelson's word, or if we accept the EC estimate in 2012, another £99.3bn. By this measure, EU membership does not seem a particularly sensible use of UK taxpayers' money.

For those who think that trade is only one of the benefits of membership, the calculation will not be possible until they attach some value to the other benefits that they claim Britain enjoys as a result of its EU membership, such as its 'global leadership role', or being able 'to walk tall' in Beijing and other places, or being able to extradite criminals more easily, or receiving EU assistance in the fight against climate change. Obviously, they have no need to confine themselves to benefits mentioned by Messrs Blair and Clegg, and might want to refer to peace in Europe or goodwill among member countries, or easier travel to member countries.

They might find it difficult to put an exact figure on one or more of these supposed benefits, and might perhaps find it easier to do so relative to one or other items of UK national expenditure in 2013. They should, however, push themselves, since if they do not they will be obliged to accept what might be called the Clegg position, after its best-known proponent. This is that the costs of EU membership need never be identified or measured, since the immeasurable and ineffable benefits of EU membership are so great that they must be worth paying whatever they may be.

Table 14 is intended to help them to assess the value of the benefits they think flow from EU membership, by giving the real or estimated direct costs for 2013, alongside a more detailed list of various items of public expenditure in the same year. They themselves will of course have to decide whether the benefit they are evaluating by reference to these domestic policy expenditures actually exists.

**Table 14:** Equivalents of the known or estimated costs of EU membership v. capital and current expenditures on various UK public services in 2013

| If this known or estimated cost was correct (in 2013)… | | …it would have covered the total UK government expenditure for that year of one or more of the following | |
|---|---|---|---|
| The annual net cash payment to the EU | £11.5b | Environmental protection | £10.6b |
| | | Housing | £9.46b |
| HMT estimate of benefit to UK exports of EU membership | £14.2b | International services | £7.95b |
| | | Agriculture, fish, forestry | £5.28b |
| | | Science & Technology | £3.60b |
| The Mandelson estimate of cost of EU regulation (4% GDP) | £66.22b | Debt interest | £48.09b |
| | | Defence | £36.36b |
| | | Public Order & Safety | £31.30b |
| | | Transport | £18.77b |
| The European Commission estimate no.2 (6% GDP) | £99.33b | Education (schools and universities) | £86.99b |
| EU cost estimate no.3 (11.5% GDP) | £190.38b | Health (NHS) | £123.39b |

Source: PESA Table 5:4 Public sector current and capital expenditure on services by function 2009-10 to 2013-14

They must also remember that, of the costs listed, only the direct payment is recoverable by the UK government in full if it were to leave the EU. It might, of course, recover more, if it did not wish to continue the same level of payments currently made to farmers, fishermen, universities and others via the EC. But it is probably best to assume that any independent UK government would continue to make these payments, and only recover the relatively small percentage that it pays to the EC for distributing them to UK farmers, fishermen, universities and others on its behalf, as well as the £11.5bn.

By contrast, the indirect costs are not recoverable by the UK government. If the UK were to leave the EU, it would not recover the lowest estimated costs of EU regulation of £66.2bn, plus the direct costs, and then be able to double its expenditure on defence, or spend seven times as much as it now does on housing. The reduction of these indirect costs would be felt by businesses and public and private services across the land. They would, so to speak, receive the £66.2bn, not the Treasury. It is possible of course that businesses might, as a result, be more efficient, and consumers and the government might benefit, but to an unknown extent, and at some unknown point in the future.

## The final consideration

Apart perhaps from those who take the view that the trade benefits are the sole benefit of membership, voters hoping and trying to make an informed assessment of the costs and benefits of EU membership before voting in the EU referendum will, it is clear, be engaged in a difficult calculation. One major source of the difficulty is the lack of trustworthy evidence and estimates of both costs and benefits.

However, we should be quite clear why it is not possible for voters to do this. It is because over the past 40-plus years, successive UK governments have taken the view that it is easier to persuade the British people of the merits of the EU, and convert them to share their enthusiasm for membership, by their own word-of-mouth recommendations, rather than by collecting and regularly publishing evidence of the impact of EU membership on the UK economy. Had any government taken seriously its obligations to the British people in this respect we would already have the following:

- Repeated, and therefore more trustworthy, estimates of the proportion of UK exports that might be attributable to the EU, and not therefore have to rely on a single Treasury estimate from 2005;

- Regular estimates of any contribution EU membership might have made to the improvement of UK productivity, and therefore not have to wonder whether it has been negligible, or zero, or negative;

- Regular assessments of the impact of FTAs negotiated by the EC on UK exports, so that voters could judge for themselves the wisdom of ceding responsibility for trade negotiations to the EC;

- Regular examination of the true indirect costs of membership, so that we would not have to choose between the reported comments of Lord Mandelson, or asides in EC documents, or the work of Batten and Congdon.

Thus far, the present government appears to be the latest in a long line of governments that have declined to provide the information which voters require to make an informed choice about EU membership. The European Commission has similarly felt under no obligation to provide information and evidence about the specific costs incurred and benefits enjoyed by the British people.

One issue in any forthcoming referendum is therefore whether any project whose officers, beneficiaries and enthusiasts have been less than diligent, over many years, in informing those who pay for it about its full costs and benefits should expect them to be willing to continue to do so. How many voters in Britain will want to stay in a club of that sort?

# APPENDIX J

## The legacy of deceit and misinformation about the UK's relationship with the European Community and Union 1957–2014

Source: The primary source used to compile this catalogue is Christopher Booker and Richard North, *The Great Deception: Can the European Union Survive?* London: Continuum, 2005. Referenced as 'B&N'.

| Date | Subject | Author | Comment & source |
|---|---|---|---|
| 1957 to date | 'The historical roots of the European Union lie in the Second World War. Europeans are determined to prevent such killing and destruction ever happening again.' | European Union Europa website | Its roots lie in the First World War, and it had considerable support across continental Europe in the 1920s, 30s and 40s. B&N 73, http://europa.eu/about-eu/eu-history/1945-1959/index_en.htm John Laughland, The Tainted Source; the undemocratic origins of the European idea, London, 1997 |
| 1960-62 | Repeated public statements European integration is economic rather than political. | Harold Macmillan | While privately asserting that entry into Europe was an act with wide-ranging political consequences, which should never be mentioned.p.217, George Ball, The Past has another Pattern B&N 107, 126 |
| 1970 | May 1970 general election. The Common Market was briefly mentioned in the Conservative manifesto It only said 'We will negotiate no more, no less.' | Edward Heath | Began negotiations immediately after election, having already taken the decision to enter. B&N 167 |
| 1970 | During negotiations, the EEC was simultaneously discussing the Werner and Davignon Reports which declared members' goals of economic and monetary union, and political union respectively. | Edward Heath and Geoffrey Rippon | Both reports were ignored in political debates in the UK surrounding negotiations. B&N 170 -172 |
| May 1971 | Secret agreement with Pompidou acknowledging the need for a common currency & expressing enthusiasm for it. | Edward Heath | B&N 175-177 |

| Date | Subject | Author | Comment & source |
|------|---------|--------|------------------|
| July 1971 | 'There is no question of Britain losing essential national sovereignty... fair and reasonable terms' of entry have been negotiated. | Edward Heath: The United Kingdom and the European Communities (White paper Cmnd 4715 July 1971). | 'Lord Chancellor, Viscount Kilmuir advised him on legal implications of entry... I must emphasise that in my view the surrenders of sovereignty involved are serious. For parliament... to give automatic force of law to any existing or future regulations made by the... Community... would go far beyond the most extensive delegation of powers, even in wartime, that we have ever experienced.' B&N 122-6, 179-80 The UK contribution was scheduled to rise to 18.92% of the entire EC budget http://www.th-eu-nit.com/downloads/TheHistoricDecision.pdf B&N 179 |
| Dec 1971 | '[O]utstanding problems on fisheries had been resolved. The Community had been persuaded of the need to protect Britain's vital interests... we retain full jurisdiction of the whole of our coastal waters up to 12 miles... These are not just transitional arrangements.' | Geoffrey Rippon, chief negotiator on entry to the EU | UK inshore fishing had already been considered 'expendable'. The UK retained exclusive control of its territorial waters only up to 6 miles, and only for a 10 year period. Even before that, British fishermen would have to comply with Community rules .B&N 180-4, 189-193,401, 413-4 From this year on, it began a long and relentless decline, though the contribution of the CFP to it has never been demonstrated. Taxpayers' Alliance, The Price of Fish: Costing the Common Fisheries Policy (2009) |
| 1974-5 | Labour government will seek 'a fundamental renegotiation'. On their conclusion, [Wilson] claimed 'its objectives had been substantially achieved'. | Harold Wilson | Nothing fundamental was negotiated or changed. The former Prime Minister Heath, and many others, declared it 'was a sham,' B&N 202-6, http://civitas.org.uk/pdf/The Prospects of EU Renegotiation.pdf Lessons from the 1975 EU renegotiation, http://forbritain.org/bfb060-historians-report-mr_r.pdf |
| 1990 to date | 'No Minister of the Crown should give agreement in the Council of Ministers to any proposal for EC legislation which is still subject to scrutiny.' | Resolution of House of Commons, 24 October 1990 | Hundreds of directives and regulations have been and are routinely written into UK law without scrutiny every year. B&N 353, 361-2 |
| Dec 1991 and May 1992 | This is a treaty 'which clarifies and contains the powers of the Commission'. The European Council has 'agreed a package of measures to reverse centralisation... The future of Europe is now based on free trade and competition... on a proper definition of the powers of the Commission.' | John Major, to House of Commons, on the Treaty of Maastricht 11 December 1991 and 20 May 1992 | Although he had prevented UK participation in some further centralisation by opt-outs of the European currency, of the Social Chapter, and refused to surrender control of immigration to the UK, his description of this Council meeting to the Hof C is wildly misleading. By all other accounts, it was a major landmark in the integration and centralisation of the EU, with a wide-ranging extension of EC competences, of the powers of European Court, and of QMV. No examples of reversing centralisation have ever been given by him or anyone else. B&N 332-342 |

| Date | Subject | Author | Comment & source |
|------|---------|--------|------------------|
| Dec 1992 | Edinburgh Council meeting said to have agreed 'a package of measures to reverse centralisation' | John Major to House of Commons 14 Dec 1992 | On the grounds that the Commission had produced a list of laws which it thought must be simplified or abolished. The major theme from Major's point of view was subsidiarity, whose practical significance then or since is difficult to identify. The main substantive issue at the meeting was the four opt outs, to persuade the Danish people in a second referendum to approve the Maastricht Treaty. Specific measures to 'reverse centralisation' are difficult to find in Major's autobiography. |
| Dec 1993 | European Council is determined to pursue 'market-oriented policies... de-regulation... a more decentralised Europe, flexibility in labour markets and reductions in social costs.' | John Major to H of C Hansard col.24 Hansard, col 68511-12 December | No evidence given, then or since, of deregulation, of decentralisation, or of reduction in social costs instituted by the EU. B&N, 351, 379-380 |
| 1994 | 84% of CBI members are in favour of a single currency. | CBI | The 84% in fact consisted of 59 survey responses. The CBI then had about 8,000 members. The CBI acknowledges the financial support of the European Union for its surveys. p.386, B&N. |
| 1995 | Cost of EU to 'each Briton was 2p per week' reported by The Observer as 'just 2p per head per year.' | David Williamson, Sec-Gen of the EC. | The EC's own figures at the time showed it was £2.45 per head per week, and £127.40 per head per year. B&N 595-6 |
| Dec 1995 | '[T]he drive to promote subsidiarity was again strongly in evidence.' | John Major to House of Commons reporting on Madrid Council | There are no examples of this 'drive', or of subsidiarity ever being used to return powers to member states. B&N, 395 |
| 1997 | On becoming PM his declared aims with respect to the EC were: 1) to secure legally binding rights to keep frontier controls, 2) to oppose the integration of the WEU with EU, since he was not in favour of bringing defence under EC control, and 3) to honour a campaign pledge and curb foreign vessels fishing for British quotas. | Tony Blair, *The Independent*, 13 June 1997 | Amsterdam meeting abolition of veto in 16 policy areas, and transfer of responsibilities to the Community Framework, Social Chapter integrated into Treaty with UK support. Start date of EMU fixed. Appointment of person responsible for Common Foreign & Security Policy aka Foreign Minister. Declined to subsequently admit publicly, or in his autobiography, that the first two of his initial aims were forgotten, and fishermen got, not a treaty change but agreement with the Commission that boats using British quotas had to land 50% of catch in British ports. B&N 412 |
| 2000 | 'Eight million jobs lost if Britain left the EU'. | *The Independent*, 18 February 2000, and Britain in Europe, a business pressure group | A grotesque misreading of research by the National Institute of Economic & Social Research. B&N 451 |

| Date | Subject | Author | Comment & source |
|------|---------|--------|------------------|
| April 2003 | 'The electorate should be asked for their opinion when all our questions have been answered, when all the details are known, when the legislation has been finally tempered and scrutinised... There is no question of any constitutional treaty going through without the express consent of the British people... Regardless of how other members vote, we will have a referendum on the subject.' | Tony Blair to House of Commons, 20 April 2003 Repeated by Jack Straw 26 January 2005, by Geoff Hoon, Europe minister, 23 May 2006, and other ministers | Blair confirms EU constitution poll http://news.bbc.co.uk/2/hi/uk_news/politics/3640949.stm When asked, three years later, if there would be a referendum, he said 'No. If it's not a constitutional treaty, so that it alters the basic relationship between Europe and the member states, then there isn't the same case for a referendum.' *Financial Times* April 2007. The Lisbon Treaty was signed by Gordon Brown on 13 Dec 2007. http://www.heritage.org/research/reports/2008/03/the-eu-lisbon-treaty- |
| May 2003 | In April 2003, the responsible minister, referring to the drafting of the European Constitution told the Foreign Affairs Select Committee, 'this process will have substantial constitutional significance.' But on 18th May he said the proposed constitution for Europe was just 'a tidying up exercise'. | Peter Hain, Foreign Office minister, UK representative at EU Constitutional Convention | 'Valéry Giscard d'Estaing, chairman of the convention on Europe's future: the European Union's draft constitution that he unveiled on May 26th presents a unique chance to set the EU's course for the next 50 years.' *The Economist*, 23 May 2003 http://www.economist.com/node/181 2391D h-A p.129 http://news.bbc.co.uk/2/hi/programmes/politics_show/3038091.stm 18th May 2003 |
| March 2004 | 'A study commissioned by the Home Office before EU enlargement in May 2004, predicted that enlargement would lead to an average annual net immigration of 5,000-13,000 A8 nationals for the period up to 2010.' (A8=post 2000 entrants to the EU) | UK Home Office | '... In total, more than 765,000 A8 workers – of whom two thirds are from Poland – have registered for employment in the UK since gaining free access to the UK's labour market when their countries joined the EU in May 2004.' Select Committee on Economic Affairs, First Report, Appendix 9: Measuring And Predicting Immigration From Eastern Europe, 2008. http://www.publications.parliament.uk/pa/ld200708/ldselect/ldeconaf/82/8 220.htm |
| 2006 | Citizens of other EU countries 'who are convicted of a serious criminal offence are deported immediately.' | Tony Blair | The UK has no legal power to do this, as Mr Blair must have known p.146, Derek Heathcoat-Amory, Confessions of a Eurosceptic, Barnsley, 2012. |
| 2007/8 | 'It's time for a REAL REFERENDUM ON EUROPE... Only a real referendum on Britain's membership of the EU will let the people decide our country's future' with a photo of Nick Clegg, the Lib Dem Leader, Sign our petition today, and return to: Real Referendum Petition, London SW1 3 NB | Liberal Democrat campaign advertisement but apparently 2007/8 | Fifteen members of his party felt they should honour this pledge and accordingly voted on 5 March 2008 to support of a Conservative motion for a referendum on the Lisbon Treaty, Clegg and others abstained. http://www.newstatesman.com/politics/2013/05/eu-referendum-leaflet-will-haunt-clegg-today; http://en.wikipedia.org/wiki/Nick_Clegg Subsequently, Clegg became a resolute opponent of a referendum. p140, Heathcoat-Amory. |

| Date | Subject | Author | Comment & source |
|------|---------|--------|------------------|
| Sept 2007 | 'Today, I will give this cast-iron guarantee: If I become PM, a Conservative government will hold a referendum on any EU treaty that emerges from these negotiations. No treaty should be ratified without consulting the British people in a referendum.' | David Cameron in *The Sun* | 'David Cameron to shed 'cast iron' pledge on Lisbon treaty' 3 November 2009 Some hours after Václav Klaus, the Czech president, signed the (Lisbon) treaty, William Hague, the Shadow Foreign Secretary said: "What has happened means it is no longer possible to have a referendum on the Lisbon treaty." http://www.theguardian.com/world/2 009/nov/03/david-cameron-lisbon-treaty-referendum |
| 2010 | 'Any proposals which involve significant changes in the relationship between the Union, the member state and its citizens should be approved in Britain through a referendum.' | Nick Clegg to Liberal Democratic Party Conference | It looks like a pledge to support a referendum on the Lisbon treaty, though everything hinges on the word 'significant', which the leader himself would decide. |
| April 2010 | 'If you elect a Conservative government on 6 May, we will... control immigration, reducing it to the levels of the 1990s – meaning tens of thousands a year.' | David Cameron in a pre-election 'contract between the Conservative Party and You' | He declined to tell the electorate that it is not possible for a UK prime minister to control immigration from other EU countries. In the year ending September 2014, there were 292,000 immigrants from other EU countries. http://www.ons.gov.uk/ons/rel/migration1/migration-statistics-quarterly-report/february-2015/index.html |
| 2014 | 'People say you'll never be able to cut the EU budget. I've cut the EU Budget... I've got a track record of doing what I say I'm going to do.' | David Cameron PM, BBC Today programme, 30 September 2014. He repeated the claim on other media outlets | At an EU Budget summit on 7/8 Feb 2013, Cameron and other EU leaders agreed a €908 billion limit for the seven-year period 2014 – 2020. This was 3% lower than in the previous seven-year period. Hence his claim. However, a few months later this decision was overturned, and the EU budget, and the UK contribution sharply increased. Source: Tim Congdon's open email 30th September 2014 quoting evidence from the Office of Budget Responsibility, the Office of National Statistics and the HM Treasury White Paper, European Union Finances, 2014 |

# Notes

## Chapter One

1   House of Lords Select Committee on the European Union (Sub-Committee B), Inquiry into Re-launching the Single Market, Oral and associated written evidence, Department for Business, Innovation and Skills, p.110, written evidence (EUSM 7) 14 October 2010:

http://www.parliament.uk/business/committees/committees-a-z/lords-select/eu---internal-market-sub-committee-b/publications/ Oral evidence was given on 24 January 2011, pp.119-137.

2   Michael Burrage, *Where's the Insider Advantage?* (London: Civitas, 2014), pp.10-11.

3   *Ibid.*, p.29.

4   *Ibid.*, p.23.

5   *Ibid.*, pp.15, 31.

6   Fabienne Ilzkovitz, Adriaan Dierx, Viktoria Kovacs and Nuno Sousa, *Steps towards a deeper economic integration: the Internal Market in the 21st century: A contribution to the Single Market Review*, by the Directorate-General for Economic and Financial Affairs, N° 271, January 2007, ISSN 1725-3187: http://ec.europa.eu/economy_finance/index_en.htm.

7   Lionel Fontagne, Thierry Mayer and Soledad Zignago, 'Trade in the Triad: how easy is the access to large markets?', *The Canadian Journal of Economics / Revue Canadienne d'Economique*, Vol. 38, No. 4 (Nov. 2005), pp. 1, 401, 430.

## Chapter Two

1   Strictly speaking, their comparison should have been between intra-Japan and intra-US and intra-EU trade, rather than comparing Japan-US or US-EU trade, so the level of fragmentation in the EU might be compared with that *within* Japan and *within* the US.

2   Fontagne, *op.cit*, p.1411. Unfortunately, they did not give a breakdown by EU member country of the decrease in border effects. This would have been extremely valuable data. In 2011 a BIS report found it 'instructive to observe the huge variation in the costs of trading across EU member states, all of which operate under a common regulatory framework. For example, based on the 2011 Trading Across Borders Survey, importing and exporting costs twice as much, and takes three times as long in the worst-performing EU member states as in the best-performing. Clearly, common rules do not generate common outcomes.' *Trade Facilitation*: UK issues. Trade and Investment Analytical Papers, BIS/DFID Trade Policy Unit, 2011, p.16.

3   Fontagne, *op.cit*, pp.1427-8.

4    Ilzkovitz *et al., op.cit.*

5    *Ibid.*, p.32, Figure 3-4.

6    As we noted above, in one case where national data is given - price compression - the impact on the UK was that prices increased far above those of the EU25 mean. This may be a gain for the process of creating the Single Market but can hardly have been perceived by the British people as a 'substantial economic benefit'. The same might be said of increased M&A activity, since the resulting economic benefits are obscure and unmeasured.

7    Evidence from the OECD databases.

8    House of Lords, *op.cit.*, p.134.

9    Without enlargement effects, Ilzkovitz, *op.cit.*, p.57.

10   GDP growth (annual %): http://data.worldbank.org/indicator

11   'A strategic review of Better Regulation in the European Union', Commission of the European Communities, COM(2006) 690 final, 14 November 2006, p.6: http://eur-lex.europa.eu/LexUriServ/LexUriServ.do?uri=COM:2006:0689:FIN:EN:PDF.

12   These figures were featured on the Better Regulation website, at least until 12 February 2012 (screen capture copy only). However, the 2010 strategic review reported that it is 'on track to exceed its target of cutting red tape by 25 per cent by 2012', but the 'estimated burden' was then stated to be €134bn. No research is cited to support either of these estimates. 'Smart Regulation in the European Union', European Commission, COM, (2010) 543 final, 8 October 2010, p.3: http://eur-lex.europa.eu/LexUriServ/LexUriServ.do?uri=COM:2006:0689:FIN:EN:PDF

13   The full data is given in Michael Burrage, 'A club of high and severe unemployment: the Single Market over the 21 years 1993-2013', Europe Debate No.4, (London: Civitas, 2015): http://www.civitas.org.uk/pdf/burrageunemployment

14   Does the current economic environment require a re-thinking of the Single Market? How should confidence in the Single Market be restored? Is the UK affected by market or integration fatigue? What role should be played by national parliaments? In order to deliver the re-launch of the Single Market, is there a need to refocus the way that the relevant measures are dealt with by the EU institutions? It also asked for evidence on tax coordination as a mechanism for driving the completion of the Single Market; the role the Services Directive has played in completing the Single Market and plans for creating a digital single market.

15   These questions were very much influenced by the topics raised in the Monti Report which had been published just before the committee meeting. Mario Monti, *A New Strategy for the Single Market at the service of Europe's economy and society*, Report to the President of the European Commission, 9 May 2010. Professor Monti's evidence to the committee preceded that of the minister.

16   To experienced observers of the House of Lords, the reluctance of its European select committee to rigorously cross-examine a declared europhile minister would come as no surprise, and my expectation that they would be ready to do so will seem hopelessly naïve and uninformed. Private Eye recently reported that 'the old committee stitch-ups continue with the usual procedures grinding to ensure the Upper House's numerous European select committees

will be staffed mainly by vigorous Europhiles'. A plea by Lord Pearson, a former leader of UKIP, for more balanced representation, was dismissed by Lord Foulkes, ('an admirer of Brussels and its gastronomy') who reportedly said: 'I had the privilege of serving on the committee for the last three years and I found it very interesting.' Referring to Lord Pearson's request he said: 'What we have heard from the noble Lord is complete nonsense, and I hope it will be thrown out comprehensively.' 'Needless to say', *Private Eye* continued, 'it was, and the main Lords EU Select committee duly includes such ardent Euro-enthusiasts as Quentin Davies, Roger Liddle and Ian Blair.' 'Called to Ordure', by Gavel Basher, *Private Eye*, 26 June 2015.

17 *Twenty Years On: The UK and the Future of the Single Market*, published by the Centre for Economic Policy Research (CEPR) and HM Government, 2012: https://www.gov.uk/government/publications/twenty-years-on-the-uk-and-the-future-of-the-single-market

18 *Ibid*, p.1. Could this possibly be, I wondered, after some sort of intra-departmental game of Chinese whispers, the source of the phrase 'EU countries trade twice as much with each other as they would do in the absence of the Single Market programme'?

19 The FCO prepared a review of all the submissions - *Review of the Balance of Competences between the United Kingdom and the European Union: The Single Market*, HM Government, July 2013. The most relevant pages on its economic benefits are pp.35-39, and in an appendix, pp.61-72, a review of the six 'main studies' attempting to quantify the economic impact of the Single Market. It includes the EC report of 2007 discussed above which is the only one 'to review the latest empirical evidence on the economic impact of the Single Market'. We must therefore assume that the 'latest' empirical evidence on the economic impact of the Single Market available to the government in 2013, was from 2007 or earlier.

## Chapter Three

1 Their grievances were aired in 'Review of the Balance of Competences between the United Kingdom and the European Union Fisheries Report': https://www.gov.uk/government/consultations/fisheries-review-of-the-balance-of-competences.

2 The CBI has received EC grants, as have some of the members of the Association of the British Pharmaceutical Industry, many members of the National Farmers' Union and of Universities UK. AB Sugar has benefited from protective tariffs for sugar beet. Two MEPs submitted papers, but their interest is self-evident.

3 Barry M Jones, a sole trader.

4 The British Chemical Engineering Contractors Association's submission to the competences review's 'Trade and Investment' chapter, available as part of the evidence, found here: https://www.gov.uk/government/consultations/review-of-uk-and-eu-balance-of-competences-call-for-evidence-on-trade-and-investment.

5 See the SWA's submission to the competences review's chapter on 'Trade and Investment'.

6   'Scotch whisky exports fall at fastest rate since 1998', *Daily Telegraph*, 22 September 2014; 'Scotch export sales dry up as US loses its appetite', *Daily Telegraph*, 1 April 2015. In these reports, the chief executive of the association called for 'support from government to beat down trade barriers and help us access new markets overseas', and later 'for more open markets and ambitious trade deals that tackle barriers to market access'. No reference is made to the EC, and these recent comments are very odd given the euphoric commendation of the EC in his submission.

7   OECD ILibrary, Monthly Statistics on International Trade. For comparisons over the years before and after 2006 when the EU FTA came into force, it is necessary to use Chile imports from the UK data series rather than UK exports to Chile, since the latter series is interrupted for some unknown reason. Chile was not, by the way, atypical in this respect. See Michael Burrage, Where's the Insider Advantage?, p.48. This study examined the growth in the value of UK goods exports before and after 15 EU FTAs came into force. They were found to have declined in 10.

8   An evaluation of the Mexico FTA is currently under way by contractors commissioned by the EC. However, the chances that it will identify the benefits for the UK seem remote, since they are asked to measure the impact on the EU as a whole.

    See Business for New Europe's submission of evidence to the competences review's chapter on Trade and Investment.

9   UK exports did increase over the year 2011/12 by some 14 per cent. This is high versus the growth of UK world services exports in that year, but not especially high versus the growth of UK exports to Korea in years preceding the treaty.

10  Their predecessor, Britain in Europe, was similarly careless and misleading in the data it published to support the case for the UK joining the euro, Burrage, *op.cit.*, pp.109-122.

11  Though negotiations of a Comprehensive Economic and Trade Agreement with Canada were concluded in December 2014: http://trade.ec.europa.eu/doclib/docs/2014/december/tradoc_152982.pdf.

12  SMMT submission to the competences review's chapter on Trade and Investment, p.2.

13  The British Ceramic Confederation seemed to have something of the sort in mind, at least with regard to legislation. 'When implementing new legislation', it said, 'the EU should carry out a full financial and economic impact analysis at an early stage, and this should be updated on an on-going basis.'

14  'Our Global Future: The business vision for a reformed EU', Confederation of British Industry, 2013, p.58.

15  The submission of the Freedom Association claimed that this had happened in the late 1990s, when 'through the work of Senator Philip Gramm, former Chairman of the United States Senate Banking Committee, and others... the EU could have had an FTA with the USA... only for it to be rubbished by French concerns.' However, this episode is not well documented in their submission to the balance of competences review.

16  The only submission which refers to the content of EU FTAs is that of the British Chambers of Commerce which notes that the EU has recently

'embarked upon a new and deeper trend by insisting that its partners adhere to EU competition policy principles as part of its deals.' In the case of Colombia and Peru, it pointed out that 'the EU even managed to bind sub-national authorities to these principles. Realistically, it is unlikely the UK alone would have been able to achieve this result alone.[sic]'

17  Hence, by the way, the large number of EU agreements with very small countries.

18  We know they didn't. See Wenfei Law, *A Practical Guide to the new Free-Trade Agreement between Switzerland and China*, December, 2013. Even if the collective clout of the EU enabled it, sometime in the future, to secure a more favourable agreement with China, the Swiss expect that their agreement will be upgraded accordingly.

19  The OECD has proposed an ISTR template. For a dated but useful commentary on this effort see http://www.astm.org/SNEWS/MJ_2011/perspective _mj11.html

20  The International Organization for Standardization is a global non-governmental organization. Formed in London in 1946, but now located in Geneva, it works through its members, 164 national standards agencies, and with the participation of hundreds of thousands of engineers and others, has created tens of thousands of standards, which are often the benchmark in trade negotiations. It was the beneficiary, royalty-free, of the patents of the most important trade facilitation innovation of all time, the shipping container, by its inventor, Malcom McLean.

21  The 10 May 2013 letter from the President of the American Society for Testing and Materials (ASTM) James Thomas, to Douglas Bell, the chief US TTIP negotiator, shows it is poised to resist any attempt by the EC, which it regards as a newcomer to standard-setting, from a small group of countries, to overturn long-standing voluntary consensus global standards. ASTM was founded in 1898. It is a private non-profit organization, open to interested persons anywhere in the world, and now has more than 30,000 members from 140 countries. Thomas drew a contrast between the 'open development process of ASTM and other US domiciled standards developers [which] allows for the direct participation of individual experts from anywhere in the world in order to reach a global consensus', while 'participation in the European standards development… is limited to European experts working to reach a European consensus.' The US view is that 'there are multiple paths to international standards', and it therefore 'encourages the public and private sectors alike to make standards-related decisions through the interpretation and application of the WTO TBT (Technical Barriers to Trade Committee) principles', while Europe 'restricts choice and flexibility' by 'officially designating' international standards bodies such as 'the International Organisation for Standardisation (ISO), the International Electrotechnical Commission (IEC) and the International Telecommunication Union (ITU)'. Moreover, it grants a 'presumption of compliance with certain European standards' which it denies to 'non-European safety standards – even when these standards are of equal or superior quality'. He calls for more openness, transparency and flexibility in the European regulatory process, equivalent to that found in the US.

22  One of the curious features of the submissions favouring the present balance of competences is while they often mention the difficulties of the plurilateral trade negotiations organised by WTO, they forget that the preliminary intra-

EU trade negotiations are themselves plurilateral, albeit involving only 28 nations, and rather easier than those of 161 WTO members.

23 According to the UN Comtrade database: www.comtrade.un.org. Its evidence is reproduced and discussed in Appendix F.

24 In 2010 UK services exports to other EU members were nearly double the size of Switzerland's. They totalled $97.6bn while the Swiss totalled $55.3bn. *Ibid*, p.31. The data for Swiss exports to the EU members is taken from the services imports by the EU from Switzerland, since Swiss services exports are not classified by destination. Their total world exports are, however, from the services exports dataset, as is the UK data.

25 According to balance of payments evidence, UK exports of financial services in 2013 totalled $62.6bn, while Swiss exports totalled $16.7bn. UK exports of insurance services over the years 2005-2013 grew by 25 per cent whereas the Swiss grew by only 9 per cent: http://stat.wto.org/serviceprofiles. Obviously, other factors are involved, most notably the strength of the Swiss franc, but we are here only looking for *prima facie* evidence.

26 Singapore financial exports in 2013 totalled $18.4bn. *Ibid*.

27 TheCityUK submission to the BOCR, p.3, *op.cit.*

The British Retail Consortium, which also supported this argument, pointed out that the European Commission has 531 trade policy officials while BIS now has only 30. It rather spoilt the impact of this contrast however, by later noting that fully one quarter of these EC officials were engaged in so-called trade defence activities, of which it was highly suspicious. The CBI also doubts whether the UK has the human resources to conduct its own negotiations, and has elsewhere warned that if it were to leave the EU, 'It would take time for the UK to first regrow the capability to negotiate FTAs and there would be a period of dislocation – perhaps for many years – while new UK bilateral deals were finalised.' p.155, 'Our Global Future', *op.cit.*

28 Since 60% of all the public procurement contracts in the US awarded to EU bidders go to UK companies, it seems likely that the UK is not devoid of negotiators with kindred skills. Commission Staff Working Document, 'Impact Assessment accompanying Proposal for a Regulation of the European Parliament and of the Council establishing rules on the access of third country goods and services to the European Union's internal market', p.30, COM (2012) 124 final, SWD (2012) 58 final: http://eur-lex.europa.eu/legal-content/EN/TXT/?uri=celex:52012SC0058.

29 'EU Reform: A view from TheCityUK', TheCityUK, November 2014

31 Other professionals in the City do not seem to have quite as much confidence in the expertise of EC officials. The Fresh Start submission cited a survey which found that 69 per cent of UK financial services professionals support the UK having a veto on future EU financial services regulation, even if at the risk of less access to the Single Market and reduced business opportunities. 'EU Fresh Start', the Fresh Start Group, 2013, p.21.

32 It has professional associations across all service industries which, unlike those in any other member country, have substantial international memberships. It has long had world-wide university extra-mural programmes which, again, no other member country has any equivalent. This means that its negotiators will likely encounter negotiators in partner countries with qualifications that match or resemble their own, and even belong to the same professional

associations. Most important of all, most of the large potential services markets either speak English, or accept it as their preferred second language, and not simply in their businesses, but also in their universities and schools.

32  BOCR submissions, *op. cit.*

33  BOCR submissions, *op. cit.*

34  It is also, of course, a member of NAFTA, the North American Free Trade Area, with Canada and Mexico, both of which are also much smaller economies than Britain.

35  The same exercise might, of course, also be conducted versus the Singaporeans or Chileans or Koreans.

36  It seems fairly clear that if the EU were really intent on extending its world trade in services, it would have long since abandoned the strategy of simultaneously negotiating services FTAs on behalf of all its members. It would instead have invited the UK (and Ireland) to negotiate and pilot FTAs with a service element, which other members could join as soon as they and the partner country were ready and willing to do so. The reasons for prohibiting member countries negotiating their own FTAs in goods are well known and widely accepted, but the case for treating services in the same manner is far less compelling, since re-exporting of services is less likely and more readily identifiable. One of the incidental by-products of this alternative strategy would be that freer international trade in services would have provided a strong incentive for member countries to eliminate the national and local barriers that currently restrict intra-EU services trade, and therefore help to bring the EU Single Market in services to life.

37  The letter of Barry M Jones, manual worker and sole trader, is once again unique, in that it is the only submission to challenge this idea.

## Chapter Four

1  It is, of course, possible that imports from other members might have tripled and therefore, even though exports declined, UK trade as a whole with other members could have doubled. The minister's claim might yet be shown to be formally correct, albeit misleading. However, before pursuing this possibility, it seems sensible to look first at the scale of export growth to see whether the known imbalance in UK trade with the EU would make a significant difference.

2  The calculations make use of the Excel growth function which instantly calculates the exponential growth curve through a given set of export values over a given set of years, in this case from 1973-1992. This can then be extended year by year to calculate additional export values, in this case for the 20 years 1993-2012. In all the cases considered below, the linear growth curve differs only marginally from the exponential, usually with a lower best fit $R^2$ measure.

3  Ilzkovitz, *op.cit.*, p.32,

4  International trade in goods and services, values and shares of merchandise exports and imports, annual, 1948-2012. Flow: Exports, Measure: US Dollars at current prices and current exchange rates in millions. Calculated in 1973 US dollars.

UNCTADstat:
http://unctadstat.unctad.org/wds/ReportFolders/reportFolders.aspx.

5   These CAGRs include of course, EU countries, both as exporters and importers.

6   In US(2012) dollars they totalled \$23.4bn per month in 2012.

7   The peak year in the case of UK exports therefore differs from that of the EU as a whole, which was 2008, most probably as a result of differences in the method of recording exports, rather than a real difference in the timing of the crisis.

8   However, it might be unwise to make too much of this 0.41 per cent growth advantage as an indication of the benefits of the Single Market, since exports to independent countries were growing at a faster rate. If, for instance, we take only ten years of pre-crisis growth, that is from 1998 to 2008, the CAGR of those to the EU is 3.69 per cent, while that of exports to independent countries is 4.90 per cent.

9   Their growth rates differed widely as may be seen from Table 5. By this measure, Switzerland seems to have benefited most from its agreements with the EU, Turkey next, and the two members of the EEA, Norway and Iceland, least.

10  However, they say nothing about how this gain may have been distributed among member countries, over how many years, or for that matter of its costs. Barry Eichengreen and Andrea Boltho, 'The Economic Impact of European Integration', Centre for Economic Policy Research Paper No. 6820, 2008, pp.31-33: www.cepr.org/pubs/dps/DP6820.asp.

11  Ali M. El-Agraa, *The European Union: Economics and Policies*, Seventh Edition, (Cambridge University Press, 2011) pp.110-112. They later refer to it as 'a political success'. Professor El-Agraa is evidently a firm believer in 'ever closer unity for Europe'. Wolfgang Munchau recently came to a still more depressing conclusion about the impact of the Single Market: '…if you look at the trend of EU-wide productivity', he wrote, 'the Single Market leaves no trace. In fact, productivity growth in the EU was in the order of 1-2 per cent a year in the late 1980s. Between 1990 and 2000 it fluctuated around 1 per cent. The average between 2001 and 2007 was 0.7 per cent, and it has averaged around zero since. It has been downhill ever since the official start date of the Single Market in 1992. Productivity trends in Britain are very similar. You could, of course, argue that without the Single Market, the situation might have been worse, but that assertion is impossible to prove. My point is that the Single Market is not visible in the macro statistics… Advocates of the Single Market might benefit from it personally, and so might their shareholders and employees. But the data are telling us a different story—that the Single Market is a giant economic non-event, for both the EU and the UK.' Wolfgang Munchau, 'Would it actually matter if we left the EU?', *Prospect*, July 2015.

12  'Our Global Future', *op.cit.*, pp. 131-151; Mats Persson *et al.*, 'What if…? The Consequences, challenges & opportunities facing Britain outside EU', Open Europe, 2015, available at:

    http://openeurope.org.uk/blog/britain-can-prosper-post-brexit-if-it-embraces-free-trade-and-deregulation; John Springford *et al.*, 'The Economic Consequences of Leaving the EU', Centre for European Reform, June 2014, p.34, available at: http://www.cer.org.uk/sites/default/files/publications/attachments/pdf/2014/report_smc_final_report_june2014-9013.pdf.

## Chapter Five

1   As discussed below, coverage differs according to the Extended Balance of Payments Services (EBOPS) classification used. Coverage of the earlier EBOPS 2002 is more complete than that of EBOPS 2010.

2   Ilzkovitz, *op.cit.*, p.32.

3   'Europe in Figures', Eurostat yearbook, section on international trade in goods: http://ec.europau.eu/eurostat/statistics-explained/index.php/Eurostat_yearbook. In 26 countries the intra-EU trade in goods exceeds extra-EU trade. The two exceptions, i.e. poorly integrated countries, are Greece and the UK.

4   *Ibid.*, section on international trade in services.

5   For example, one recent study by the Centre for European Policy Studies (CEPS) for the EC 'attempts to take stock of the remaining gaps or deficits in intra-EU market access obligations in services, and the related deficits in the proper functioning of the internal market for services. If they are taking stock of its gaps and deficits, one can only assume that they have located the Single Market in services itself. The Cost of Non-Europe in the Single Market II - Single Market for Services: http://www.europarl.europa.eu/EPRS/EPRS_STUDY_536354_CoNE_Single_Market_II.pdf. It appears from its website that 77 per cent of CEPS funding in 2015 came from the EC or some other EU institution.

6   Wolfgang Munchau, 'Would it actually matter if we left the EU?', *Prospect*, July 2015.

7   The New City Initiative, a trade group of boutique fund managers, conducted research to discover how 'the "free market" of Europe was working for the asset and wealth management industry... We were amazed to discover that there is no "free market" for financial services.' After giving examples of the costs and national barriers that prevent the free movement of capital, he came to the view: 'If the UK left the EU (assuming trade treaties and other issues can still be negotiated), I do not believe that it would make any difference at all to the ease – or difficulty – of trade for our industry in the EU.' Dominic Johnson, 'I've fallen out of love with Europe until the trading rules are changed', *Daily Telegraph*, 27 September, 2015.

8   Switzerland, Iceland and Turkey could not be included since they still report their services exports to the OECD only in their total services exports to the world.

## Chapter Six

1   Motor cars and car parts are the preferred example of EU enthusiasts. But then it happens to be one of the few sectors which is still protected by a relatively high tariff barrier. For analytical purposes, it is therefore necessary to distinguish the impact of this tariff from the SMP per se. There is a certain irony in the choice of this industry. By most accounts, the UK is supposed to have pushed the EU, and the Single Market in the direction of free trade, but this industry is a case where it has evidently failed to do so. And it does, of course, rest the case for continued British membership of the EU on the continuance, even permanence of its protective tariffs, which is disconcerting.

2    Ilzkovitz, *op.cit.*, p.48. The diagram following the comment indicates that extra-EU imports' share in apparent goods consumption in the EU increased from 9 per cent in 1986 to 15 per cent in 2003, while intra-EU imports' share rose from 20 per cent to 24 per cent, and domestic consumption fell from 71 per cent to 62 per cent.

3    Harry Flam and Håkan Nordström, 'Trade Volume Effects of the Euro: Aggregate and Sector Estimates', Institute for International Economic Studies, Stockholm University, Seminar Paper No. 746, June 2006, p.10. The size of the differences between euro and non-euro countries varies with the control group. When they use a larger control group of OECD countries instead of the three non-euro EU countries, the benefits of the new currency for trade between euro countries increased to 15 per cent while the trade from non-euro countries to the euro countries increased by 7.5 per cent.

4    Richard Baldwin, 'The Euro's Trade Effects', European Central Bank, Working Paper Series No.594, 2006, pp.42-47.

5    *The Economist*, 22 June 2006: http://www.economist.com/node/7085268

6    *Financial Times*, 3 July 2006.

7    Michael Burrage, forthcoming publication in the Civitas Europe Debate series.

8    Richard North first drew attention to the many so-called EU rules that originate in numerous global standard-setting organizations in 'The Norway Option', The Bruges Group, 2013. For a detailed examination of how Norway, despite being a non-member country, has been able to influence upstream a number of rules that were later adopted by the EU, see Jonathan Lindsell, *The Norwegian Way: A case study for Britain's future relationship with the EU* (London: Civitas, 2015), pp.30-39.

9    The scores of Poland, Austria, Greece, Finland and Italy are more than double those of The Netherlands, the most open of the 50 countries measured. The UK comes second: http://www.oecd.org/tad/services-trade/sector-notes-services-trade-restrictiveness-index.htm.

10   'On the result of the performance checks of the internal market for services (construction, business services and tourism)', Commission Staff Working Document SWD (2012) 147, Brussels, 8 June 2012.

11   Copenhagen Economics, 'Economic Assessment of the Barriers to the Internal Market in Services', Final Report, January 2005; Hildegunn Kyvik Nordås and Henk Kox, 'Quantifying Regulatory Barriers To Services Trade', OECD Trade Policy Working Paper No. 85, February 2009. Copenhagen Economics observed that 'we do not distinguish between intra-EU and extra-EU firms (for three reasons)... Firstly, we could not find sufficient data on the extra-EU barriers. Secondly, most of the barriers will be the same for foreign intra-EU firms and extra-EU firms... Thirdly, it will often be difficult in practice to distinguish between extra-EU and intra-EU firms. When a firm is established in one Member State, it automatically becomes an intra-EU firm, and it will face exactly the same legal barriers as other EU firms. For example, Coca Cola is in reality an intra-EU firm, because Coca Cola have subsidiaries in EU Member States.'

12   The BIS paper on trade facilitation, 2011, fn 9 *supra*. listed surveys by the World Bank, the World Economic Forum, and private bodies such as the Global Express Association. Global accounting and consulting firms regularly produce

surveys of the trade, compliance and other costs in various countries for their clients and the Canadian government has a triennial regulatory compliance costs survey, www.statcan.gc.ca. See also for the use of such surveys Nordås and Kox, op.cit.

12 'Trade Facilitation', BIS, 2011, p.11, fn 9, *supra*. They still differ widely. The Global Express Association produces a customs capability index (CCI) based on measures of specific customs procedures. The most recent index, based on 2013 data, shows that despite their common regulatory framework, the scores of EU countries, even of founder members of the Single Market, are nowhere near identical. While Portugal and Greece score 5.5 and France and Belgium 6.5, the UK scores 10. By this index, the UK has the world's most efficient customs procedures. The authors also note that 'the impact of improving CCI is consistently stronger for exports than for imports, with the average being 4.8 per cent to 6.0 per cent.' pp.66-74: http://global-express.org/assets/files/Members-Library-2/GEA_FinalReport_040315_STC.pdf.

# Chapter Seven

1 Ken Clarke, 'It Is Time To Put The European Case More Strongly', *Social Europe Journal*, 31 January 2013.

Transcript of a speech by Ken Clarke at the launch of the Centre for British Influence through Europe on 30 January 2013: http://www.social-europe.eu/2013/01.

2 At an Institute of Directors dinner on 28 November 2013, Sir John Major pronounced confidently: 'We would lose inward investment – ask Japan or Korea, or even America.' See: www.johnmajor.co.uk/page4370.html. He had earlier predicted to a Chatham House audience that, if the UK left the EU, 'foreign-owned companies would then migrate to the EU'. Sir John Major, The Referendum on Europe: Opportunity or Threat?, Chatham House, 14 February 2013, see: http://www.johnmajor.co.uk/page4364.html. Evidence that that contradicts him may be found at pp.79-80, 172, Burrage, *Where's the Insider Advantage? op.cit.*

3 'Lord Mandelson: Britain 'bonkers' to leave European Union', Angela Monaghan, *The Guardian*, 1 April 2014:

http://www.theguardian.com/business/2014/apr/01/lord-mandelson-britain-bonkers-leave-european-union

4 Baroness Ashton, who briefly succeeded him (2008-2009) did not do so either. Credit for this elementary reform seems to be due to the Belgian trade commissioner Karel de Gucht (2010-2014).

5 Oliver Kamm, 'Future UK prosperity depends on remaining in the EU. Here's why', *The Times*, 2 April 2015. He then repeated, with a similar blithe disregard for published evidence, the argument of Sir John Major that 'big manufacturers would move out' if the UK left the EU.

6 Hugo Dixon, *The In/Out Question: why Britain should stay in the EU and fight to make it better*, Scampstonian, 2014, p.91

7 Office of the United States Trade Representative, Executive Office of the President, Free Trade Agreements:

https://ustr.gov/trade-agreements/free-trade-agreements.

8    Burrage, *op.cit.*, pp.45-52.

9    Its reliability rests on the fact that Congdon endeavoured to select the most trustworthy independent sources when piecing together his estimates rather than on his own research. Tim Congdon, 'How much does the European Union cost Britain?' UK Independence Party, London, 2012: http://www.timcongdon4ukip.com/docs.

10   And the data collected by the EC is sometimes inadequate. To give a very relevant example in the present context, the European Parliament only began to consider how the performance of the Single Market might be measured in June 2014. European Parliament, 'Can we measure the performance of the Single Market?' June 2014:

     http://www.europarl.europa.eu/RegData/etudes/ATAG/2014/536298/IPOL_ATA(2014)536298_EN.pdf.

11   One pressure group, British Influence, has decided to make the importance of 'our biggest market' its primary, or perhaps sole message for remaining a member of the EU. Since every country in the world could also define the 28 nearest countries as 'our biggest market', it is not clear how and why this helps the case for a political union. However, it does make for a very simple message that may persuade those who have little time to consider the issue.

12   Green Book: https://www.gov.uk/government/publications/the-green-book-appraisal-and-evaluation-in-central-government; Magenta Book: https://www.gov.uk/government/publications/the-magenta-book.

31   For the full text see *The Guardian*, 23 January 2013. The online version is at https://www.gov.uk/government/speeches/eu-speech-at-bloomberg. Bloomberg HQ seems a curious location to put the argument that the Single Market is 'the principal reason' for UK membership of the EU. Over recent years, many of the interviewees on its television channel have spent considerable airtime reflecting on the dismal state of the EU economy.

## Chapter Eight

1    The country identified as the destination of FDI may not be its ultimate destination but simply the home of special purpose entities in which funds are parked before investment elsewhere. Since there are a lot of SPEs in the Netherlands, it is usually referred to as 'the Netherlands effect'. The issue is discussed in Burrage, *op.cit*, pp.83-90.

2    Only one contributor to the Foreign Office balance of competences review, NATS (National Air Traffic Services) raised any questions about the EC's negotiating priorities. It complained that the 'rationale for selecting countries for EU agreements is unclear', and noted that 'several important emerging markets seem to be missing from the information supplied, for example both Australia and New Zealand'. The answer to the question, and the complaint, appears to be that Commonwealth countries are not in the neighbourhood of the EU, and not in the Mediterranean.

3    'And rather than allowing Europe and America to look inwards and stand apart we will promote a new transatlantic economic partnership as we seek a strong pro-European pro-Atlantic consensus in Britain.' Speech by Gordon Brown to the 2003 Labour party conference in Bournemouth, reproduced in

the Guardian online, 29 September 2003: http://www.theguardian.com/politics/2003/sep/29/labourconference.labour1.

4    CBI, 'Our Global Future', *op.cit.*, p.59.

5    Here are a few examples. The founding document of the Single Market, the Cecchini Report, is a series of predictions of increases in growth and employment derived from the HERMES and INTERLINK models of the EC. 'Commission of the European Communities', 'Europe 1992: The Overall Challenge', Brussels, 1988, Paolo Cecchini *et al.*, SEC (88)524. http://aei.pitt.edu/3813/. The staff report discussed above (IIzkovitz, 2007) used the MIRAGE model (*op.cit*). The much-cited Barry Eichengreen and Andrea Boltho study mentioned above relies on a number of estimates from models. The UK BIS report, with an imported team of French analysts, relied on the MIRAGE model to make predictions about the benefits of further integration of the Single Market for the UK and other members in Economics Paper No. 11, 'The economic consequences for the UK and the EU of completing the single market', Vincent Aussilloux *et al.*, 2011; the five reports of 'The Cost of Non-Europe in the single market' ('Cecchini Revisited') have used various models to estimate the gains that might be made by 'further completion' of the Single Market in the free movement of goods, of services, digitalization, public procurement and consumer legislation. Their final estimate is that 'potential economic gains... range between 651 billion and 1.1 trillion euro per year, equivalent to between 5 per cent to 8.6 per cent of EU GDP.' 'The Cost of Non-Europe in the Single Market: An overview of the potential economic gains from further completion of the European Single Market of EU GDP, PE 510.981, EPRS European Parliamentary Research Service, September 2014: http://www.europarl.europa.eu/.

6    One model that was particularly influential at the time of the euro debate in the UK and elsewhere is now known to have made wildly mistaken predictions. The model created in June 2014 for the Centre for European Reform made claims about the trade benefits of EU membership which can be shown to be highly implausible. It is examined in Appendix G.

7    Among the more notable are: 'How much legislation comes from Europe?' Research Paper 10/6213, Oct 2010; 'Leaving the EU', Research Paper 13/42, 1 July 2013; 'The economic impact of EU membership on the UK', SN/EP/6730, Sept 2013; 'The European Union: a democratic institution?', Research Paper RP14/25, April 2014; 'Migration Statistics', SN/SG/6077, February 2015. All can be found at http://www.parliament.uk/briefing-papers.

8    For copious documentation of the abuse of those opposed to the UK joining the euro by *The Guardian, The Observer* and *The Independent*, see Peter Oborne and Frances Weaver, 'Guilty Men', Centre for Policy Studies, 2011.

9    Eurobarometer, the European Commission's public opinion analysis body: http://ec.europa.eu/public_opinion/index_en.htm.

10   According to the Europa website, the principle of subsidiarity is 'fundamental to the functioning of the European Union'. It means that the Union can only act in matters that cannot be better performed at national and local level. See also: Judgment of the Court in Case C-233/94.

11   After the first attempt, an EC spokesman said: 'A legal assessment of the opinions issued by national parliaments did not lead to the conclusion that the principle of subsidiarity has been breached.' EurActiv:

http://www.euractiv.com/socialeurope/ec-drops-regulation-right-strike-news-514793. For a first-rate short account on these cases see Hugo Brady, CER, 'The EU's 'yellow card' comes of age: Subsidiarity unbound?', 2013: http://www.cer.org.uk/insights/eus-yellow-card-comes-age-subsidiarity-unbound.

# Appendices

1   The report can be found here: http://ec.europa.eu/economy-finance/publications/publ ication784_en.pdf

2   There are no citations to support the wide agreement about the positive impact of the euro on trade integration.

3   This paragraph is from a section called 'international dimension', p.48.

4   *Ibid*, p.51.

5   *Ibid*, p.53.

6   *Ibid*, p.30.

7   Although comment is reserved till the next section, one cannot help but observe, in defence of the authors, that this last phrase, is exceptional, and by far the silliest in the entire report, p.49.

8   *Ibid*, pp.50-51.

9   'This is', they say, 'because integration and competition enhancing reforms have had disciplinary effect on firms' pricing strategies, the increased trade with higher income economies, improved production quality and the Balassa-Samuelson effect associated with the income convergence have pushed price levels up.' p.38.

10   *Ibid*, p.55.

11   The text says 'in 2006', but they might better have conveyed their meaning by saying 'by 2006' or over the period 2002-2006. These gains are, as they point out in a footnote, measured in 2002 prices.

12   'Review of the Balance of Competences between the UK and the EU: Consultation on Internal Market: Free Movement of Goods', Scotch Whisky Association comments:

https://www.gov.uk/government/uploads/system/uploads/attachment_data/file/278520/Scotch_Whiskey_Association.pdf

13   United Nations Commodity Trade Statistics Database (COMTRADE) HS code 2208.30: www.comtrade.un.org.

14   'Pensions giant: Brexit would be 'disaster' for UK', *Daily Telegraph*, 24 March 2015.

15   John Cridland, 'In or out, Britain has to play by Europe's rules', *The Times*, 4 July 2013; OECD Dataset: Trade in services - EBOPS 2002 European Union (27 countries) Total Services Imports.

16   Though it also mentioned a number of minor reforms it would like to see. 'Our Global Future: The business vision for a reformed EU', CBI, 2013. This continued on the theme of the severe limitations of Swiss agreements with the EU on services, pp.144-145, still without mentioning its higher rate of export growth.

17   *Ibid.*, p.59,

18   The EC 2007 Staff Report examined in the text, section 1.

19   GDP growth (annual %): http://data.worldbank.org/indicator.

20   It predicted cumulative gains over 5 or 6 years of between 4.25 and 6.5 per cent of GDP, and substantial improvements in productivity. 'Europe 1992: The Overall Challenge', Commission of the European Communities, SEC (88)524 final, Brussels, 13 April 1988.

21   See for example the frequent references to the 'organization of exchange of best practice' in the Treaty of Lisbon, pp.82, 83-84, 86, 150, *Official Journal of the European Union*, C306, Volume 50, 17 December 2007.

22   Itaqa Sarl, 'Evaluation of the economic impact of the Trade Pillar of the EU-Chile Association Agreement', Final report, for the European Commission, Directorate General for Trade, March 2012: http://trade.ec.europa.eu/doclib/docs/2012/august/tradoc_149881.pdf.

This refers to itself, and is referred to elsewhere by the EC, as 'the first wide-ranging, ex-post assessment of a specific bilateral trade agreement carried out at the request of the European Commission.' p.29, *ibid*. There was an earlier six-nation assessment, which seems to have been considered a pilot. Copenhagen Economics, 'Ex-Post Assessment of Six EU Free Trade Agreements, An econometric assessment of their impact on trade', prepared for the European Commission, DG Trade, February 2011: http://trade.ec.europa.eu/doclib/docs/2011/may/tradoc_147905.pdf.

23   Burrage, 'Where's the Insider Advantage?' pp.45-52

24   *Op.cit.*: http://www.cer.org.uk/publications/archive/report/2014/economic-consequences-leaving-eu

25   'We took data on the total value of goods traded – exports and imports – between Britain and 181 countries between 1992 and 2010.' p.24; 'We took panel data from 181 countries between 1980 and 2010.' p.91.

26   In reality, as is well-known, exports have consistently been rather less than half of UK trade with the EU, the mean proportion over the years 1999-2014 being 46.23 per cent: http://www.ons.gov.uk/ons/rel/international-transactions. This means that the model's calculation of the amount of UK export growth attributable to EU membership was rather less than 55 per cent. Whether this is a significant difference in this analysis may best be judged after examining the figures below. So as not to keep the reader in suspense, it isn't. And if it had been for their calculations, the authors would surely have pointed it out.

27   'EU membership and Trade', HM Treasury, 2005, pp.6-7: http://www.hmtreasury.gov.uk/d/foi_eumembership_trade.pdf

28   Excerpted from: http://trade.ec.europa.eu/doclib/docs/2013/july/tradoc_151669.pdf.

29   From: http://www.brandtschool.de/home.html.

30   From: http://www.oecd.org/daf/fin/private-pensions/Biographies-G20-OECD.

31   House of Commons Library, 'The economic impact of EU membership on the UK', SN/EP/6730, 17 September 2013.

32 From a research point of view, his contributions to the debate are particularly disappointing since he is a former eurocrat and MEP and for many years wrote columns in *The Guardian* which is widely thought to be the paper of choice for social scientists. One might have expected him to have access to, and to use, the very best research to support his beliefs. For that reason, I read, with the help of www.journalisted.com, every single article he has written on the EU since 2001. As far as I can discover, he has never quoted any empirical evidence to show the benefits of EU membership. Instead he has referred to its 'untold benefits' and rather annoyingly, to its 'immeasurable benefits'. The only empirical evidence he chose to cite or discuss in 198 articles in various newspapers since 2001 were on 9 March 2004, to show immigration from Eastern Europe would not be an issue for the UK, and on 15 December 2005, to show that UK per capita income and productivity trailed behind several other member countries.

33 The 12 countries were Austria, Denmark, Finland, France, Germany, Greece, Ireland, Italy, Netherlands, Portugal, Spain and Sweden. Belgium and Luxembourg were omitted because in 1972 they reported as a union, and no UK exports to them were recorded. The GDP figures used were those prepared by Samuel H. Williamson, 'What Was the U.K. GDP Then?' *Measuring Worth*, 2015: http://www.measuringworth.com/ukgdp/. The figures given in Office for National Statistics, 'Economic Trends Annual Supplement No. 32', 2006 Edition, ed. David Harper, Palgrave Macmillan, 2006, plus the 2005-2013 figures from the ONS, give slightly higher percentages but a similar downward trend, from 19.83 per cent in 1973 to 17.10 per cent in 2013. The Williamson figures indicate the peak year for integration with the EU was 1974 when the proportion topped 22 per cent. In 1979, it was just over 20 per cent, and in 2007 and 2008 just under.

34 'EU membership and Trade', HM Treasury, 2005, pp.6-7: http://www.hmtreasury.gov.uk/d/foi_eumembership_trade.pdf

35 The CAGR of UK productivity over the years 1993-2013 was 0.07 per cent above the OECD mean, and it is this difference that might, conceivably, be attributable to EU membership, if we had good reasons and evidence to make this attribution.

36 Converted at the average exchange rate for 2013 of €1.16 to the pound: http://www.x-rates.com/average.

EU Revenue & Expenditure 2007-2013: http://ec.europa.eu/budget/financialreport/2013/foreword/index_en.html.

37 The balance of payments figure prepared by ONS show the UK paid £12.9 billion to the EU in 2013. However, HM Treasury has presented different figures on different occasions. These have been examined in some detail by Congdon who concluded that 'a fair assessment has to be that the annual net cost – meaning the direct fiscal cost – to the UK of its EU membership lies in the vicinity of £10 billion to £13 billion, roughly ¾ per cent of GDP.' pp.14-18, Tim Congdon, 'How much does the European Union cost Britain?' UK Independence Party, Seventh edition, 2014: http://www.timcongdon4ukip.com/docs/EU2014.pdf.

According to the revenue and expenditure xl. page of the EC Financial & Budget Report for 2013, the total sum received from the UK was €20,841.1m from which must be subtracted a fee paid to the UK for collecting duties *et al.* of €852.9m and EU expenditures in the UK of €6308.3m. This left a net contribution of €13,319m which at the mean exchange rate of €1.16 to £1 for the calendar year of 2013 equals £11,481.9m or £11.5bn: ec.europa.eu/budget/.../revenue...expenditure.../.

38  Jean Eaglesham and Frederick Studemann, 'Mandelson calls for Brussels to pick fights', *Financial Times*, 8 November 2004: http://www.ft.com/cms/s/0/bf97ad9a-31c2-11d9-97c0-00000e2511c8.html#axzz3cT0ItOZK. The quotations marks, it should be noted, refer to the FT report, and not to the words of Lord Mandelson.

39  Jonathan Lindsell, 'Does the EU impede the UK's economic growth?' Civitas, Europe Debate series, No.2, 2014.

40  The EC did not date its estimates, but given that it is referring, in 2012, to a target 'by 2012', one guesses that it is referring to the study which it had conducted in 2009. Commission of the European Communities, 'Reducing Administrative Burdens in the EU', Brussels 28 January 2009: http://ec.europa.eu/governance/betterregulation.

41  Tim Congdon, 'How much does the European Union cost Britain?' UK Independence Party, Seventh Edition, 2014, p.7: http://www.timcongdon4ukip.com/docs/EU2014.pdf.

11.2.16